Never Let Go

Dhrahent F. Pean

Flagg Mountain Press
13 Louisburg Square
Centerville, MA 02632

$\mathcal{T}$he letter was postmarked in Hyannis. Inside was a check for two hundred dollars and a note that read: "Friday, five PM. Phone 362-9865 if you can't make it." The address followed, and a signature that looked like T. Porter.

I didn't know anyone named Porter. I didn't know more than five or six people on all of Cape Cod, for that matter, hadn't been there except to go fishing since I was a teen-ager and spent a summer, one memorable summer there. Was this a job offer? If it was, why no details?

Two names appeared at the top of the check: Thomas D. Porter and Florence Paxton Porter - husband and wife, presumably.

Only two days earlier I'd returned to the top floor apartment in my building on Revere Street, Beacon Hill, after a case that had dragged on for over a month and had kept me living in rooming houses while I played tag with a psychotic bad-check artist in the Back Bay. It was good to relax again, sit around and read and listen to music. But you don't meet the mortgage payments that way.

How long would it take to drive to the Cape? Over an hour, if I remembered correctly, though Friday traffic could be brutal on a clear fall afternoon. Better allow for that.

I showered, then dressed conservatively, locked up the apartment and went to see if my car was still where I'd parked it the night before. You never know now. The Resident sticker is a help - at least you don't often have to park miles away anymore - but without a deliberate mental note of where you put it last time it can be infuriating trying to remember where your car is. And even when you do remember, there is always

1

a niggling worry that a tow truck, or car thief, or some drunk driver may have whisked it away or side-swiped it.

I live in the city because that's where most of my work is. I do private investigating. My contacts are here, as well as people who know about me and will recommend me; quite a few, too, who would like to drop my corpse into the polluted waters of Boston Harbor - if they could find out where I live.

The Toyota was where I'd left it on Myrtle Street. No scratches. No new dents.

I drove to my bank and cashed the check, that way if I got to the Cape and didn't like whatever was waiting for me I'd be two bills ahead for the afternoon jaunt. Might have supper in some fancy restaurant, take a room in a motel and go swimming, breathe some ocean air. On the other hand, there might be a job in this. Wait and see.

About five miles this side of the Sagamore Bridge the line of cars ahead of me stopped moving. We went bumper to bumper, lurching, stopping, inching forward and then stalling again.

I'm a pretty patient guy, as a rule. A lot of my work involves just sitting and waiting. But there is something about traffic jams that riles me. We keep building more and more roads so that more and more cars can get to more and more places. But when you get there, there's no place to put the car. And half the time you can't reach the place without getting past some bottleneck like the Callahan Tunnel or the Sagamore Bridge. Good cheap public transportation would save more money and time and lethal frustration than all the multi-billion-dollar highways in the country. But the sacred cow of America is everyman's automobile. Would I want to go without mine?

It took almost an hour to cover those five miles. I was in a mean mood by the time I crossed the Canal - felt as if I'd earned the two hundred already.

Luckily, the address I wanted was off route 6-A and easy to find. A long dirt drive with willows along it led away from the road past a small freshwater pond, red cedars, bushes that looked like blueberry. This was nice land. After the soot-covered brick and trash-strewn streets of Boston the Cape was some kind of island paradise. Small wonder so many people came here every chance they got.

I parked behind a battered pick-up truck. Beyond it stood a house that was only a couple of years old, all angles and glass, overlooking the marsh. Money? Yes. Taste? What you get if you pay enough. The creek came up to a small private dock at the edge of a grassy slope. Not bad.

I didn't see any bell so I lifted the big brass knocker and let it whunk down two times and waited.

The door swung open on a man in his late fifties, big. Lots of ropy muscle under flesh just beginning to lose its tone. He had on a faded blue sweatshirt and gray slacks. His feet were bare.

"Yes?" he asked, as if I'd come to the wrong place.

"I'm Jeeter," I said.

His eyes walked over me. "You're small," he said.

The fact is, I'm five foot seven and that has its advantages.

I said nothing.

"And you're black."

"Any more trenchant observations?" I asked.

His eyes narrowed. He wasn't used to back-talk.

"We were told you're the best," he said, and it was obvious he was thinking someone had been full of shit.

I looked past him down a dark hallway with Daumier prints on the walls. Voices. Men's voices, from a room behind him. Maybe he was waiting for me to give him a little more lip. I let him wait.

3

"You might as well come in," he said at last, "since you're here."

I stepped inside and he shut the massive oak door behind me.

"Straight down the hall into the salon," he said. Ritzy - salon yet. At least he didn't try to say it in French.

I knew he was watching to see how I moved. I went ahead of him and entered a room that was actually terraced so that seated anywhere in it you would have an unobstructed view of the salt marsh and the harbor beyond, only tempered glass and wide overhanging eaves between you and the September scene.

Sunlight, from low in the west behind us, lay like a warm ochre coverlet on the beiges and browns before us.

The men in the room stopped talking when I came in. After a glance at me everyone turned to look through the glass where I was gazing. For the time it takes to breathe deeply once, no one spoke, then a narrow long-shanked fellow in a three-piece suit stood up and nodded at me. He didn't offer to shake hands.

"You must be the specialist we sent for," he said. "I'm Seelye. Attorney. You've met Tom Porter, whose charming house this is. And this is Frank Huck" - he gestured - "the third member of our group."

The three gave me cold looks. There was mistrust there. I didn't mind that. I mistrusted them too. But there was the old familiar supercilious looking-down-the-nose conviction of in-born superiority. All three seemed to have it.

Blue-bloods. Yankee stock from way back. Money. The upper class. Sometimes I wished I could strip these types naked and turn them loose at night on Blue Hill Avenue and see how long their patrician noses stayed clean.

4

"I think we better check him out very carefully." It was Porter who had spoken. I'd rubbed him the wrong way. They all continued to stare at me. No one had suggested that I sit down.

"Tom, we had the word of three other parties that this guy is tops. We haven't got time to run any other checks." Huck was speaking. "Let's get down to business."

"I'd side with Porter," the lawyer said. "Frankly, this doesn't look like our kind of person."

I could have been a piece of meat on the butcher's block with three customers deciding maybe they'd like a different cut.

"While you girls are twitting each other," I said, "I think I'll just mosey along. The kind of trouble you people get into you probably deserve."

I took a step toward the hall but Huck was out of his chair. He was a hefty bouncing 210 at least. It looked relaxed and natural when he was seated but it was all rubber and sinew when he was on his feet. He was the kind of man you'd find on a thirty-foot boat south of Nantucket, alone, two lines out, left Wychmere at three AM, wouldn't get back until dark. And after an eighteen hour day on the water, with nine to a dozen thirty-pound bass in the box, he'd drive all the way home to Lincoln or Waban and still get to work the next morning fresh as an April crocus.

"Mr. Jeeter," he said. "I'm sorry. Forgive us. We're on edge. We need help and we're not used to asking for it. Sit down, please. Can I get you something to drink?"

There was a lot of fibre in this one. No dummy. Energy to burn but he wouldn't waste it. Quick. "I don't drink," I said, "but I'll let you tell me what your problem is."

I sat on a Hitchock chair that was next to a tilt-top table. Huck propped a haunch on the arm of a leather easy chair. He

5

gave his partners a look that as much as said - Let me handle this.

"Someone's trying to buy us out," he said, speaking directly to me. "We own about ninety acres, among us, all contiguous, between the main road and the marsh and out to the harbor. Last spring a man came to each of us in turn and asked if we would consider selling. We didn't say Yes and we didn't say No. We tried to get an idea what he had in mind and what he intended to offer. I guess both sides played it cagey. He told us nothing and we didn't let on to much more. He went away.

"About a month ago another man appeared. He said he represented a certain Mr. Assiz who intended to buy our property. Intended! Could we work out an agreement? Seelye and Tom and I put our heads together and decided to tell him No deal. He said he was prepared to give us a check for one million dollars American. We told him No, No deal. He said: 'Please think it over seriously. I will phone you in a week.' He phoned here seven days later. Tom answered and said we were definitely not going to sell."

"There was a long pause," Tom said, taking over for Huck. "I thought maybe the line had gone dead. Then the man said: 'You are making a mistake,' and hung up. That night my barn burned to the ground."

All three men were looking at me then. I've watched a lot of men come face to face with coercion for the first time. Sure they've heard threats, maybe used threats themselves, but mild ones. How many times, though, have they carried them out?

But when the ordinary person is told to do something, or else, and the 'or else' the next day is murder or arson, the first reaction is disbelief. Tom Porter and Huck were looking at me, still incredulous. Seelye seemed more interested in what my response would be.

"You've been to the police?" I asked.

"Of course."

"And what was their response?"

Tom answered. "They said an old barn like mine, full of things that burn quickly - marsh hay, discarded furniture, a tank of oil and one of gasoline for the machinery - what did I expect? Rudimentary wiring could have been faulty. Rats could have gnawed through the plastic or salt air could have corroded old BX cable. There was no way to be certain. They said they'd keep their eyes open but it was obvious they weren't going to do a thing."

"You think the fire was set."

"I don't much believe in coincidences." Tom said it as if I was dumb to ask.

"How many days ago was the fire?"

"It was Wednesday night. This is Friday. I guess you know that."

"Have you heard anything else?"

Seelye was still standing, his back to the windows. "Nothing," he said.

I turned to face him. "If the fire was set in order to put pressure on the three of you, then there'll be another contact. They phoned you once so they might do that again. You could put recording devices on your phones. That might pay off. Money, I assume, is no object."

"Money is always an object," Seelye said. "We do not intend to be pushed around. Neither are we going to spend money recklessly."

He probably thought he was a shrewd one. I could see he was the kind, though, who would niggle over details and lose sight of the larger issues.

"If I decide I want this job," I said, "it's two hundred dollars a day plus all expenses. Is that too reckless for you?"

7

Huck stepped between us again. "We know what you charge," he said, "and it's not unreasonable, considering the results you usually get. We'll put tapes on our phones. Can we count on you to help us?"

I needed the money and it was my kind of job. Also, Huck was the kind of man I could get to like, maybe. The other two were a different breed. They were going to be trouble.

"All right," I said. "Get me a plot plan of the land you own so I can walk around it and see what this is all about. Then I'll need a place to stay. There must be an extra bedroom in this house. I can move in here, be on top of what goes on, and save you what a motel would cost. Is that okay, Mr. Porter?"

Tom was about to protest but Huck once more got between us. "That seems like a very good idea," he said. "I'll fix a room in my place too, so you can alternate. That way you'll be right on the property all the time, if that's what you want."

That suited me fine.

There were no more objections, at least they weren't spoken.

I turned to Huck. "Maybe you'll show me the way to the local police station," I said. "It's a good idea to report in any time I take on a job in an area where they don't know me. I think, though, that I may know the Chief here, if there hasn't been a change."

Huck had a dusty Bronco in the driveway. After we got into it he swung around the pick-up truck and my Toyota and we headed for the station.

"Why do you think someone wants your property?" I asked.

Huck kept his eyes on the road. He sat straight, both hands on the wheel. We were traveling at a steady thirty-five miles an hour.

"That's what really has us worried," he said. "I met both of the men who came around before the phone call. They were not nice types and they knew nothing about buying or selling real estate. That was not their field. When I mentioned possible title problems, neither had any idea what I was talking about. They'd been sent out to *get* the property and as it developed they intended to do so any way they could. I have a feeling someone wants to take over this tidal area and turn it into a resort. It's easy to destroy what nature had needed thousands of years to create. A hotel complex, gambling, night spots - if that's what someone has in mind, it would be a disaster."

"You may be up against a syndicate. It could be smart to yield."

Huck turned to look at me with disgust. "Is that the kind of help you want to give us?"

"I think you should know that this game could get very rough. Barn burning may be the last and gentlest warning you'll get."

"That's why we sent for you."

"I'm not an army, Mr. Huck. Suppose they doubled the offer they made you?"

"I don't need any more money," he said.

I'd never heard anyone say that before. "What about your partners?" I asked.

He hesitated. "They might be tempted," he said. "I don't know."

"Another thing," I said. "Aren't there all kinds of building codes and DEQ permits and zoning provisions that would get in the way of anyone coming in here to put a resort, or anything else, on the edge of the marsh?"

He looked at me again. "You don't think that sort of thing can stop big money, do you? This is a small town. It's full of hungry people. Anyone says Jobs, Investment Money, Increased Land Values, Tourist Build-up - all the businessmen in town'll put pressure on the ones that run the town (and half of them are in real estate or some related business) and pretty soon a way'll be found to circumvent the troublesome regulations."

He was right. I'd seen it happen a dozen times in other places.

By then we'd reached the station. Huck parked out back and we went in. The Chief was there. He was the same man I'd run into three years earlier.

At that time a kid named McPherson had been commuting to MIT. About once a month he'd steal a new car, drop it at a chop shop in Dorchester and pay off another hunk of his tuition loan that way. The Chief was sure it was someone from his town but he was getting nowhere. One of the insurance companies got hit three times and hired me. I nabbed the kid, closed the shop, collected my fees and made a friend.

"Jeeter," the Chief said, smiling, something he rarely did.

He was a hard-nosed, all-business cop. He never slept. He was the highest paid town official and a lot of people didn't like that but he'd been running his department for a long time and no one could have taken his place.

"What brings you here? Did Huck talk you into chasing an arsonist?"

"The arsonist may be ready to try some other tricks, Chief," I said.

We shook hands. He was about my size and had taken the same kind of crap I had all my life about being a runt. If he hadn't been white we might have been brothers.

"I'm gonna be staying in Porter's place or at Huck's for a while," I said. "I'm still licensed to carry. Anything that comes up, I'll let you know. How's McPherson doing?"

The smile was gone.

"Some of the local do-gooders are beginning to chortle," he said. "The kid was studying mechanical engineering, you know. The judge put him to work in a garage and he turned out to be a real whiz. He's made restitution and lately he's been putting in two days a week at the airport earning over twenty dollars an hour - almost as much as he made stealing cars. They say he'll turn into a model citizen."

I wasn't as sure of that as others might be. Crooks and alcoholics have a way of lapsing. But McPherson had been earning an honest living for a while at least. It was a lot better than keeping him in jail.

"Were you able to find out anything about the two men who first approached Huck and Seelye and Porter?" I asked.

The Chief shook his head. "Porter had a license number on the second one," he said. "It led nowhere. Anyone can rent a car nowadays. Unless we have make and model and color - even then - it's almost impossible to trace a vehicle that's not owner-operated. I think the smart criminals carry phony plates so they can change them just before coming into a new area on this kind of caper. Rental companies have certain model cars that are in demand. A smart crook rents a car like a thousand others. He gets it out of state maybe. He switches plates. He's shown fake credentials when he took it. Even if we had engine number and mileage, we'd still probably not be able to nail the guy. The number Porter gave us belonged to a retired judge who lives in Marblehead and drives a Mercedes. The Mercedes was in Ontario the day Porter took the number."

Huck was standing by the door. I looked at him. "It's another indication that we're dealing with real professionals," I said. "These aren't people we're going to scare away by stamping our feet."

"They've got to show themselves sooner or later," Huck answered. "We could pretend we're ready to deal."

"And then what?" the Chief asked. "The principals won't come to the bargaining table. Some flunky will show up with corporation papers. We can't arrest an employee just because maybe he represents someone who perhaps had something to do with attempted intimidation."

"Have you any inkling, Chief," I asked, "who might want ownership of the property?"

He took his time about answering. "It's only a guess," he said, "but any choice spot on this northeast coast would be ideal as a center for gambling interests. That's what it smells like to me. But a casino, an international crowd, luxury accomodations - this town would be transformed. The kind of money you'd see here would buy control. I'd be put out to pasture - with a generous 'pension' if I'd take it - and a whole new police force would take over. Just about every man has his price. Nobody's ever tempted me yet so I don't know what I'd do if the occasion arose. But I think I'd rather go down fighting than sell out, no matter what was offered."

Those were my sentiments too. And I'd been offered money. Many times. The only thing it ever did to me was increase my determination to fight.

What had Huck said? "I don't need any more money." Maybe he was as obstinate as the Chief and I. I was nearly ready to believe that he was.

$\mathcal{T}$he plot plans showed Porter owning 41.3 acres in the general shape of a wavy-edged rectangle. The main road was the base line on all three properties. Seelye had a strip in the middle, 19.8 acres. It wasn't very wide and it twisted and turned with the creek bed, but it extended way out into the harbor. Huck's holding was 29.7 acres, more or less square.

Early morning. The sun just over the tips of the dunes on the other side of the harbor striking the goldenrod where I was walking out from Porter's house, purple loosestrife to my right standing brilliant and regal against the yellow-green of marsh grasses.

What was the name of that camp counselor the summer I spent out here? Was it Ferguson? He was a scrawny older man with legs as thin and long as those of a Daddy Longlegs. Strong, though. He was always walking us out into the marshes. He only needed to take a long step over the ditches, straddle half of them, and then swing us kids over from one side to the other. Maybe that was half the fun of it. But he told us things I've never forgotten, like how very few flat surfaces exist in nature. Water lies flat if there's no wind but land surfaces almost never do. A salt marsh is an exception. At eye level before me, like a green-brown sea, the marsh was an unbroken horizon against the dunes on the far side of the harbor.

Twelve white herons, egrets maybe, dropped out of the sky in front of me and vanished into creek meanders I couldn't see. A strong sweet odor of briny corruption rose from clay and slime exposed by a falling tide.

I followed the edge of the marsh - cattails and phragmites, arrowwood and black cherry. A broad arm of water came up to Porter's dock.

It wasn't hard to imagine a hotel here. There are ways to do anything now. The creek could be widened. A golf course could be put in since the dock was three hundred yards from the road. How about a casino on Huck's land? And a fancy restaurant, of course. Power boats. Golf carts. Bug zappers. Dogs. Pesticides. Lawn fertilizers. Drunks and gamblers and high-priced whores. Loud speakers. Flood lights at night. The stink of cigarette and cigar smoke and fried food and exhaust fumes and people.

A breeze carressed the grasses and waves moved on them, the marsh breathing soundlessly, undulating.

I could visualize a helicopter pad out there. Underground storage tanks for aviation fuel leaking. How about a radio tower? A microwave antenna? A satellite dish?

Could it happen? No doubt it could. But there was going to be some opposition. I could promise that.

A canoe came around a bend in the creek. I stepped onto the dock. A woman was paddling. She came alongside and I steadied the canoe as she stepped out. We lifted the canoe onto the dock together.

"I'm Flo Porter," she said then. She held out her hand. "You must be Jeeter."

We shook. Her hand was strong. Salt and sand were crusted on it. She had a basket of quahogs and a rake with her. She was wearing shorts and old sneakers and a tattered tile-red sweatshirt.

"My husband said you'd arrived. Is the room all right?"

"It's fine," I said.

She was a lot younger than her husband, closer to my age than to his. Her face was wide with high, almost Indio, cheekbones and her gaze was straight into you, no nonsense and no false criteria. I liked her just as much as I had disliked her husband.

"Let me carry the basket," I said.

We walked toward the house together. "Those will make a casserole for supper," she said. "I hope you like shellfish."

I said there were few things any better.

"Have you had a look around?" she asked.

"Only the edge of the marsh."

14

"Let's drop the quahogs in the kitchen and then I'll show you the property. No one else is ever up before eight. I'm glad of a chance to talk with you when no one else is around."

She had something on her mind. We put the quahogs in the refrigerator and went out again. She showed me the burned barn and Seelye's creek where there was only a kind of fisherman's shack. "He's fixed it inside," she said. "It's got everything he needs for his comfort whenever he uses it. Which isn't very often.

"His father owned his piece of land. The old man was one of those cussed independent types who never get along with anyone. Always had a dog, though. It went everywhere with him. Old Seelye married in his middle years and had one son. The wife took off with the baby about a year later. Went up to Boston and must have found someone else to take care of her. Seelye got an education and went for a law degree and then came back here. When his Dad died he got the property. We assume his mother died long ago but he's never said so. He's unmarried. Has a modern house in town. His practice is mostly torts. Once in a while he comes out here and spends a week in his shack. Alone."

"He seemed right at home in your house yesterday."

"He and Tom get along pretty well. They play poker together with some of the other men in town. Tom likes Seelye. I'm not sure just why."

We had come to the edge of Huck's property. It was mostly cleared land with stone walls marking its boundaries. A three-quarter Cape was the main building, set way back from the road but facing it. On the brick central chimney, which was painted white, was the date 1757, in black cast iron. As we walked toward the marsh an ell and a patio came into view at the rear of the house and it was easy to see that the owner preferred this side and the open expanse of estuary it dominated. A barn that had been well-maintained stood near the

15

edge of a forest of cattails, a manure pile steaming to one side. From within came the unmistakable sound of a horse stamping its feet, telling his keeper to wake up and bring him his breakfast.

"Huck's wife died of cancer of the pancreas three years ago," Flo said. Her voice was not the same. "He's only just showing signs of getting over it now. Theirs was one of those marriages you hear about sometimes, a meeting of equals. Two vital people who were different in a hundred ways and valued every difference just as much as the primordial difference between male and female. He loved her the way every woman wants to be loved."

There was passion in the way she spoke. She turned to face me. "Yes. You understand me, don't you. I don't mind admitting it. Huck is no hero. No superman. He's just a good decent person. But he found the one woman in a million for him and he was the one man in a million for her. They had the kind of union the rest of us can only dream of."

"Will Huck marry again?" I asked.

"He needs someone."

"Are you thinking of leaving Tom and taking the place of Huck's wife?"

"You've put your finger right on it. No one can ever take her place. Sure I've thought of it but I know how those two were together. I've seen how he looked at her. I'd know if he ever looked at me and found that I didn't measure up."

It was what she had wanted me to understand, some of it anyway. Three men and one woman, the woman married to the wrong man. Four people thrown together as neighbors and now linked tightly by a threat from the outside. One of the men a loner. The property worth a fortune.

"Did you see either of the two men who came looking to buy the land?" I asked.

"I didn't even know they'd been here." she said. "Not until afterward. I'm a marine biologist and spend a lot of my time at Woods Hole."

"You have your own car, I suppose."

"It's the blue Datsun you probably saw in the drive."

"I don't want to alarm you," I said, "but it might be through you that pressure could be brought to bear. Could you arrange to travel with someone until this matter is settled?"

"You think these people might try to abduct me?"

"It's a possibility."

"But what good would that do them? Then if they got the property we'd know who they are."

"Maybe there'd be no way to prove a connection."

"I'd be able to identify someone."

"You'd probably be dead, Mrs. Porter."

She hadn't thought of that. It shook her. "Can people get away with something like that?" she asked.

"Organized crime gets away with just about anything, every day in the week."

She was turning it over in her mind. "I could ask Sam Prebble to drive me," she said. "He makes the trip every day. We've swapped rides often enough."

"When we get back to the house, let me phone him and set it up," I said. "I'd like to let him know what to watch for."

We started back, following the flood-tide line where thatch lay as much as a foot deep. When we jumped a ditch a great blue heron went up close by, his hoarse rasping voice trailing after him, legs dangling, neck stretched straight out until he got into the air. Some ducks catapulted up after him, their voices nasal and querulous.

Flo stopped and watched them. "Black ducks," she said. "A hundred years ago, at this time of year, the sky would be

17

darkened by flocks of migrant blacks and pintail and teal. Shorebirds, too, came by in numbers unimaginable today. Even twenty years ago there were bass in the Bay - old timers like to say you could walk on them there were so many. Shellfish - oysters, scallops, little necks, steamers, sea clams - there was an abundance here once that seemed limitless. We're looking at the final stragglers now. A few more years and there may be little left. Only swarms of people, dirty greedy murdering people."

Her anger was like a beacon, a fire in her ready to break out and consume her enemies.

"And now some combine wants these ninety acres so they can poison it too. They'll have to kill me to get it."

I believed her, but the kind of people we were up against wouldn't care if they murdered her. I didn't want that to happen.

*A*bout ten AM Huck went in town to pick up his mail. Twenty minutes later he came back. He drove into the Porter's driveway going a lot faster than was usual for him and tore up five feet of gravel as he braked to a stop.

"Look at this," he said, when Flo and Porter and I came out to see what was up.

He handed us a sheet of paper. The message on it was typed in capital letters without punctuation.

WHEN READY TO SELL RUN REAL ESTATE AD IN CC TIMES SAYING ITS YOURS BOX 999 YOU HAVE THREE DAYS

18

The envelope it came in had been mailed in New York City on Wednesday.

"I didn't pick up the mail yesterday," Huck said. "It was probably there then."

"I don't like this," Porter said. "Next thing, they may try burning my house."

Did it occur to him that anyone present might be in danger? His wife, for instance?

"Is there any point in turning this over to a lab?" Huck asked.

"I'll take it in to the Chief," I said. "But it won't tell us anything we don't already know."

"I'm gonna phone Seelye," Porter said. "He should know about this. Maybe he'll have some ideas on what we should do." He disappeared into the house.

"What do you think, Jeeter?" Huck was standing just to my side, eyes squinched almost shut, jaw clenched.

"I don't like getting pushed, Mr. Huck. If this land were mine I'd never let go. But you people are the ones who need to decide. Whoever wants this place is going to keep on trying to get it. It looks as if they're going to give you another warning. Will it be arson again? Will someone get hurt? Can we be waiting in the right place at the right time and stop them?"

"Maybe we could make them change their minds," Huck said. "They can't want a lot of publicity. Suppose we let the press know about this?"

"And have crowds coming here? A crowd would provide cover for them."

"But any subsequent attempt at coercion would get coverage and public opinion would be against them so that if they ever forced us to sell they wouldn't be able to do anything here. They'd be out in the open."

"You were the one yesterday, Mr. Huck, who explained to me how easy it is for big money to buy its way clear. Also, people forget. And we mustn't forget that these people can wait. We're not dealing with just one hungry small-time crook. This looks like an organization."

Porter came back outside. "Seelye's coming over," he said. "He thinks we should deal. He might have the right idea."

I saw Flo Porter looking at her husband. The contempt in her eyes would have sent a sensitive man cringing into a hole. He didn't notice. "We are not going to give in," she said.

"We'll think this over and then decide what is wisest and then we'll do it, Flo." Porter didn't like her having a say in it. Was she on the deed to his acreage? I'd have to find out.

"Well, I'm not selling." There was something final about the way Huck said it. And he was not just siding with Mrs. Porter. He seemed to have made up his mind, for whatever reason, and it didn't look as if anything was going to change that.

"Let's hold off on the decisions until Seelye gets here," Porter said. "Come on inside. He'll be here in a few minutes."

We went into the big salon. Huck sat where he could look down toward the dock. Flo Porter settled onto a sofa. Their eyes didn't meet but their awareness of each other was almost palpable.

Tom Porter paced. Then he said, "Anyone want anything to drink?" There were no takers. "Well I do," he said. He went out and came back two minutes later with a glass in his hand. The pale amber liquid was probably scotch.

When Seelye arrived, the tension in the room only increased. He snatched the note out of my hand as I extended it to him and he hardly seemed to read it. "These people mean business," he said. "We better think about doing it their way."

"That's easy for you to say." Huck was speaking. "All you've got is a strip of creek bed and a shack which you hardly use."

Seelye was still breathing heavily from his hurried trip here but he was as haughty as ever. "That shack, as you call it," he said, "has had a lot of improvements."

"You don't live there, Seelye. It isn't your home."

"What difference does that make? Didn't my father live there for his entire life? I could be just as sentimentally attached to it as you are to your holding."

"But you aren't."

"Look," Tom said. "I'm pretty attached to this place too. I'll never own another spot like this one and I'm getting kinda old to begin supervising the building of another house this elaborate, but maybe we can get these people to up the ante. They talked cash, too. There's always other land for sale when you have the money."

"Don't count on it," Flo said. "Ninety acres in a location like this is just about non-existent."

"So we'll find smaller parcels."

"And we'll come out of it unharmed," Seelye added.

"Don't you care what happens here?" Flo asked. "Don't you care if this incomparable portion of God's earth is turned into a honky-tonk haven for gamblers and pimps?"

"Frankly, I couldn't care less," Seelye said, "as long as we get fair market value for what we own."

"Fair market value be damned," Flo said. "We control something here which is unique for its size and its importance. We have a responsibility here. This is not some mass-produced plaything that we're trading. This is a link with all life forms on this planet - a salt marsh. It can be destroyed. It cannot be remade."

"You're a lawyer, Mr. Seelye," I said. "Couldn't you draw up papers making provision that all of you can remain here during your natural lives, tax free perhaps, but that at your deaths the property will pass in trust to the Town, or the Nature Conservancy, or to some other entity, to be preserved as is, etcetera? Then no one could touch you."

Porter and Seelye stared at me in disbelief.

"And give it away?" Porter said. "Are you nuts?"

"Speaking for myself," Seelye said, "I'd just as soon dispense with all further so-called 'assistance' from you, Mr. Jeeter - or whatever your real name is."

"And room and board for your stay here can be deducted from anything we decide we owe you," Porter said.

Flo was on her feet then. "What kind of cheap shortsighted fool are you, Tom Porter?"

He raised his hand and was going to belt her. I stepped in and caught his wrist. He started to plant his feet to throw a left at me so I took his right thumb in my fist and bent it down and around until is snapped.

He let out a scream and went to his knees. I let go.

"What did you do to me?" he wailed. He was looking at his twisted hand.

"You've got a dislocated thumb," I said. "If you'd hit her I would have pulled your whole arm out of its socket and wrapped it around your neck."

"Whose side are you on, anyway?" Porter asked. He was slowly getting back to his feet.

"You hired me and you're stuck with me and judging by the way you act you need me more than you'll ever admit."

Seelye had backed away. There was pure hatred in his look but he was a coward. He wasn't going to risk another chance of ticking me off.

"Give me the note," I said to him. "I'll take it to the Chief and see what kind of patrol he can set up."

$\mathcal{M}$y Tercel was in the driveway. I got in a drove toward the center of town but stopped when I saw a pay phone next to a restaurant that advertised 'Lobster in the Ruff.'

I called Jerry Frohock in Boston.

Jerry was a friend from the time we first met each other in grade school in Cambridge and found out that if we stuck together we could lick any combination of roughnecks in the school or neighborhood. Later we had some scrapes with the law and twice we burgled homes in Arlington and got away clean. I don't know why we both didn't wind up in crime. Maybe it seemed too easy.

Jerry was a whizz at math. Very early he started figuring odds on all sorts of events and made a name for himself among gamblers. Now he had an office downtown full of electronic equipment with teletyped information being fed to him twenty-four hours a day. Bankers, stock brokers, fund managers, sports buffs, buyers for international corporations, Vegas operators, politicians - a truly heteroclite crew often chose to check in with him before moving on anything. He didn't send bills. If his advice didn't result in a profit, he expected nothing (unlike so many leaches who claim a fee whether you win or lose). When his advice paid off he wanted one per cent of any gains realized. He'd seen a couple of checks that equaled my annual income.

"Haven't you retired yet?" I asked when he picked up the phone.

"Hey, Jeeter. Where are you? You in town?"

"I'm on the Cape, Jerry, and I've got a question."

"Make it a hard one. I'm tired of the easy kind."

"I don't know if this is an easy one or a lulu," I said, "but I'm wondering if you've heard anything to indicate that some-one wants to set up an operation down here? Maybe some-thing like what's in Atlantic City?"

"That's the kinda thing someone is always thinking about."

"This is going to involve some large sums of money to get started."

"Large is only a relative term, Baby."

"We're talking one million just as a first offer on the land only, Fatha."

"Let me put out some feelers," Jerry said. "Naturally you'd like the answer yesterday."

"No later, anyway."

"Call me back this evening. I'll be here until ten, at least."

"Don't you ever go home to your family?"

"They appreciate me more, the less they see of me."

"Seriously, Jerry, how come you haven't retired?"

"What for? I'm havin' too much fun right here."

*T*he Chief wasn't at the station.

A young cop at the desk said he was at the Courthouse but was due back any minute. I said I'd wait. The young guy wasn't sure what to make of me. He was about twenty-three with a sunburned face and big meaty hands. I was ready to bet he'd been a commercial fisherman until he got this job. He looked down at the report he was writing and then back at me.

"Something you want to know, Son?" I asked.

"No Sir," he said. "Well, maybe I should ask what you want to see the Chief for."

"Maybe you should."

"Well...?"

"Well what?"

"What do you want to see the Chief about?" He was beginning to be more sure of himself.

"Suppose I told you I'm from the Regional Office of the Commission for the Suppression of Discrimination Against Cod Eaters?"

He stood up. He was well over six feet and weighed about 225. "It could be the Chief isn't going to want to see you," he said.

"Is he an anti-Cod eater?"

The Chief strode in just then. He took one look at the rookie cop and shook his head. "Pay no attention to this joker, Tim," he said. "Come on in my office, Jeeter, before you get my men all worked up."

We went into his office and he closed the door. "That kid's gonna be a good cop someday," he said. "He's a slow learner but he's got a good manner and he's an impressive figure. I hope you didn't confuse him. What's on your mind?"

I handed him the note in the original envelope. "Too late for prints?" he asked.

"There won't be any," I said.

He read the note carefully. "Contact in New York," he said. "Someone here watching the local papers. Arsonist for hire. Legmen. This is an organization all right. How'd your clients react?"

I told him.

"You may be out of a job by the time you get back there."

"Could be," I said.

"We'll take you on here anytime."

"On a cop's pay I'd die of starvation."

"I don't want to see these people hurt."

"A couple of them are pretty tough."

"I don't want to see them sell out either."

"That's what would hurt the town, isn't it?"

"I was born in this town," the Chief said. "I've lived here forty-three years. When the environmentalists and bird freaks and snail darter types first started making noises I didn't think I cared for them much.

"We had gypsy moths crawling in the windows one year and there were actual skidding accidents where the caterpillers were so thick on the roads the surface turned to slime. Those people wouldn't let us spray. Lot of us didn't like that. But you know, I'm beginning to understand them.

"Nature's been solving problems a lot longer than we have. She doesn't worry much about minorities or equal pay or the handicapped and the elderly, but she comes up with ways to solve problems and they work.

"The marshes and the dunes and the brackish borders of upland, the sweet spring water we still have here, these are all threatened now. *We* are the problem now and Nature hasn't found the way to control us yet. I'd like to see the natural beauty of this place preserved as long as possible."

Flo Porter had said things along the same lines. I still had the taste and the color and the sound of the morning marsh vivid in my memory. These people had them in their blood. From way back. I was beginning to envy them.

"Can you find a way to keep extra men watching the Huck/Porter/Seelye property?" I asked.

"I'll see that someone cruises by a couple of times each hour if the week-end isn't too busy."

"Monday night may be the crucial time."

"Monday's almost always quiet. I'll put someone on it midnight to dawn. You tell him where you want him when he shows up."

"One other thing," I said. "Huck's wife died three years ago. Did they have any children?"

"Two boys. They must be almost thirty now."

"Where are they?"

"One got a job in Texas. Houston, I think. He's married. Hasn't been back here since his mother died. The other one is an odd ball. They say he's real smart but he never settled down or had a steady job. Half the time his Dad doesn't know where he is."

"And the Porters don't have any children?"

"They have one child. A girl. She's mongoloid. Institutionalized. Mrs. Porter visits her once a month. Tom won't go to see her."

I thought that might explain a lot of things about their relationship.

"Were you thinking someone might get kidnapped?" the Chief asked.

"I'm trying to anticipate how anyone would put pressure on these people. Porter and Seelye are ready to cave in now. Huck isn't. And he and Mrs, Porter seem to have an understanding."

The Chief studied my face without commenting. He was filing that one away.

"Is Mrs. Porter on the deed to the property, do you know?" I asked.

"You'd have to check at the Registry. Unless you want to ask Mrs. Porter."

"I think I'll find out on my own," I said. "Thanks, Chief." I was ready to leave.

"I know it's a long shot," I said, "but if anyone on the force spots outsiders in town, strangers, muscle, unfamiliar vehicles - you know what I mean?"

He nodded. He'd already thought of that.

*A*t the Registry of Deeds I got help from an elderly gentleman who was sitting alone at a table by a window. He had the look of those canny old codgers you find in the courts who pass their time in the halls of justice, finding their entertainment there and slowly learning a great deal about the law and how it works. He was in his eighties but he was as mentally alert as any teen-ager - maybe more so. His only handicap was his hearing but I swear he could read lips and maybe minds too.

"Would you know how to look up a piece of property?" I asked him.

"Just might," he said. His eyes walked up me from my shoes to my dark pants, to my Iceland sweater, to my black face and he smiled. "Checkin' up on some local folks, are ya?"

I think he already knew where I came from.

Two legal raptors at the next table had glanced at me too. They had their heads together but were uncertain what I might be doing in their vicinity. "I need to be sure whose names are on the deed," I said to the old man.

He nodded. I gave him the names. In less than ten minutes he led me to the book and page I needed and it showed that Thomas P. Porter et ux, Florence Valerie Porter, née Spahn, were indeed "tenants by the entirety of a certain parcel of land, being 41.3 acres, more or less, and situated..."

So Flo Porter's signature would be required on any transfer of title and there was little likelihood that she would put it there of her own free will. How was someone going to get around that? I could think of only one sure way.

The old gent was squinting at me. I thanked him for his help.

"Somethin' don't set well with you, seems like," he said.

"Nothing is ever as simple as you'd wish." I answered.

He nodded. "Could tell you plenty about that," he said. "But I won't."

$\mathcal{9}$ spent most of the rest of that day familiarizing myself with the ninety acres that someone wanted.

Huck's old Cape was a beauty. He told me I could wander all through it if I wanted. Nothing was locked. So I went through it from top to bottom, or vice versa.

There was only a crawl space under most of the ground floor but a root cellar beneath the dining room held a forced hot water heating system, an oil tank and an array of shelves that had been designed to hold canned things from a garden. Only empty jars lined them now.

Wide pine boards, downstairs, dark with age and linseed oil, were mostly covered with oriental rugs, not the usual patterns, but ones that looked far eastern to me. The furnishings were predominantly early colonial.

You could tell that a man lived here alone. The insides of closets and cabinets were neat, almost too neat, but things used or often needed were out where they could easily be reached, like the bed that was made with the pajamas lying on the spread.

On the bureau in the master bedroom upstairs was a photograph of the wife he had lost. It had to be she. Maybe it was a snapshot he took of her and had enlarged. Her left arm was raised holding short auburn hair away from her eyes as she looked up at the photographer. The wind was blowing. She half smiled. The mouth was wide and generous, the eyes far apart, the look penetrating. Was she a beauty? I couldn't say, but it seemed likely she had been a woman who, once known, no man would forget.

Smaller photos of two young men were undoubtedly the sons, one dark and serious wearing tie and jacket, the other laughing, fair, dressed in faded jeans and a tank top. Was he the drifter?

Huck came into this bedroom each evening. Did he look into those three pairs of eyes each time and remember them, say something to them silently, wonder where each was and where the years had gone?

He'd been a wanderer himself, he told me. Navy. Merchant Marine. Then importer, where he'd made his money. Now he sold marine hardware. Had a shop in town where he spent a lot of his time.

There was an attic. I climbed into it, up a rope ladder that you pulled down from a hatchway. Steamer trunks were lined up under the eaves with boxes and cartons of old clothes and toys and crockery; books, magazines, photograph albums, furniture no longer used, crates of shells someone had collected, boat models, suitcases marked "Drapes" and "Linen" and "Correspondence" - the detritus of a family's sojourn here.

A small window at each end of the attic overlooked fields and roads in one direction and marsh and harbor in the other. Wasps had nested in the rafters but all was tight and dry. The men who built these old houses, using ship's timbers and parts of other old buildings, had been real joiners - not the three-days-to-frame-it speed-kings of our times.

Seelye's shack was locked. I could have jimmied a window to get inside but there was no reason for doing that. And he'd made it clear that he'd give me not a nickel and wanted nothing more to do with me.

Through the fly-specked glass I could see a recliner chair aimed at a TV, copies of Playboy and Hustler on the floor, saucers and glasses and used pizza cartons on side tables. There was a makeshift kitchen and toilet. The cabin made me wonder if Seelye was a periodic drunk. It had the air of a place where a man could hole up long enough for a bender. A spot no one would visit. No phone and no callers wanted. What would his place in town be like? I'd have to see that one too.

The Porter house I already knew. It was ultra-modern, enjoyed every comfort, had been designed by a first-class architect and yet lacked warmth.

The couple that lived there had separate bedrooms. Any ardor they had ever known had cooled and this chill had permeated their dwelling.

Tom Porter had told me to get out. Flo had asked me to stay. Was it because I was attracted to her that I remained? I think that was part of it, but she was also the most likely target for the people who wanted the property, if things started to get rough. I wanted to stay close to her if that was going to happen.

31

Tom Porter had a bedroom in the north wing. He had his own bathroom. I'd only seen that part of the house once. Tom seemed to have been active in tennis and golf. There were cups he had won on a stand in his bedroom and there were signed photos of golf pros and tennis greats as well as several ball players. A shot of Ted Williams fly-casting was prominently displayed.

Tom's money was inherited. He'd never had to work. Sports had been his life. Maybe he'd been fairly good once.

Flo's quarters were in the opposite wing. I'd sat talking with her there when Tom and Seelye got through telling me I was fired. She said she and Huck would pay me, as agreed, and I should stay on until this thing was settled.

"I want you in the house," she said. "My husband can't put you out if I say not to. We need you."

It was not a healthy position to be in. I remembered an Italian army buddy who told me: "*Fra moglie e marito non si mette un dito* - Between husband and wife one puts not a finger." Well, I was in between. Not just part of me either.

They'd given me a guest room upstairs with a private bath. I had a deck, too, from which I could see all ninety acres except for one stretch of main road.

"I want to thank you for stopping Tom," Flo had said. "He's never struck me, but he would have in there if you hadn't prevented him. I guess I shouldn't have said the things I did, not in front of you and Huck and Seelye, but I never thought he'd raise a hand to me. We've come a long way from those first months together."

She was standing by a window, looking out, a woman who had certainly held nothing back in love, any more than she had in her work. She was the kind who decided to do a thing and then gave herself to it totally.

"Are you married, Jeeter?" she asked.

32

I told her I had been.

"And you're divorced now?"

"Sort of?" I said.

"Separated?"

"We never actually married. We lived together for two years. I considered it a marriage."

"But for some reason it didn't work." Flo had turned and her intense gaze was on me. She seemed to be drawing thoughts out of the back of my head. "Were you already in this line of work?"

"I was just getting started. Two and three nights in a row I wouldn't get home. Not everybody paid."

"And it was dangerous. Hardly a young woman's dream of love and security. Did she walk out?"

"It just fell apart and one day she found someone else."

"Have you stayed in touch?"

That was something that puzzled me about myself. "Yes," I said.

Most of the people I'd known gave little importance to old friendships, ties, close relationships. I didn't understand that. I felt that love, and the bonds of intimacy, deserved the same loyalty one owed to persons respected and deserving. Was it a quirk of mine?

"You still love her, don't you," Flo said.

It was true. I still thought of Linda as *the* woman in my life. There had been those two years when everything I did or thought or wanted was for her. When we were together, nothing else had importance and when I was working all my efforts concentrated on a future together. Then one day she was gone. She moved in with a construction worker, a hard hat, a big shrewd tough lumbering guy who owned a brick building in Roxbury and was smart about money. He made top pay and he worked regularly. I found out where they lived and went to see them. He was ready to fight. Maybe he could have taken me. But I doubt it. Only I didn't want to hurt him because I could see they were happy together.

I'd been back from time to time. Jonah didn't like to see me coming but he didn't tell me to stay away. If Linda had shown signs of unhappiness I guess I might have made a move. She was still as lovely as ever, in my eyes. They had two teen-age boys now. Wild kids. I wondered if I'd ever have any children. By whom? What they'd be like?

*H*uck's barn was the only other structure on the properties. Since Porter's barn had been burned it was not unreasonable to fear that Huck's might be next. I didn't like the thought that the horse could be cremated. There is something about the terror of animals trapped in a fire which disturbs me almost as deeply as any violence that can be done to a human. I wondered if there was some way to protect the horse, just in case.

"Could the door to his stall be left so it would open with only a nudge?" I asked Huck when he came home in the afternoon.

"We could close it with a pin," he said. "No bolt. Matter of fact, even with no kind of catch, as long as it didn't swing open by itself, he'd stay inside. And if he got out he wouldn't go far."

"This is a beautiful animal," I said.

"My wife loved horses," Huck said. "Especially Morgans. She rode daily when she was alive, until almost the last week.

I think this fellow still hopes to see her come out to him in the morning. There's a kind of disappointed look in his eye when he sees me enter the barn. I exercise him each day. It's good for me too. An early morning routine that forms a link with the past and keeps my motor running."

"Is there any particular route you take when you ride each day?"

"I suppose there is," he said. "You think I should vary it?"

"It couldn't hurt and might help. You could alter the time a little too, if that's possible."

"The horse may resist."

"I'm sure you can overcome that. And use the ride to check on anything that looks out of place or suspicious. One other thing. Do you own any firearms?"

"I've got a shotgun. Used to take a few ducks in the fall."

"How about a rifle?"

"Only a twenty-two. Woodchucks and rats were a problem in the past."

"You might get both weapons out and make sure they're in good order. Keep them handy."

He understood. He fixed the door to the stall by simply leaning a plank against it from the outside. The barn door was always left ajar that time of year anyway. Of course someone with arson in mind could bolt both doors on leaving. There was nothing we could do about that.

Farm equipment, feed, an old Nash Ambassador up on chocks, lumber and a stack of firewood filled the barn. It was a quiet cool place with the good smell of horse and hay in it. No oil or gas was stored here. Huck told me he'd always paid Porter for what he needed. Now that Porter's barn was gone he'd have to get fuel in town. He didn't need much anymore though. A yardman came in once a week. He could bring anything that was required. Huck mucked out the horse stall each

35

day himself. You could tell - most physical activities pleased him. And the affection he felt for that horse dictated that no one else should care for it.

By sundown I knew the property almost as well as its owners did.

Any approach across the marsh would have to be on foot and the countless ditches and creek arms there would make walking very difficult. There was a tide differential of nearly fourteen feet, so many of the ditches were ten feet deep with clay sides as slippery as wet glass, muck and ooze at the bottom into which you'd sink to your knees if you slipped, trying to jump across them.

Where the creek came up to Porter's dock someone could get close, unperceived, in a canoe, as Flo had done. Maybe a larger craft could come in, motor cut, on a rising tide, but then any getaway would be slow, in a canoe, or noisy, under power.

The main road was the logical place from which trouble might come. With a third of a mile of total frontage there were a dozen places where a car or a truck or motorcycle could stop on a curve or behind a clump of trees and let someone off. Traffic was steady there - tourists, locals, fishermen, delivery vans, cyclists, buses. At night it would be more sporadic, but at night, under cover of darkness, a vehicle traveling without lights would be well nigh invisible.

At nine o'clock I called Jerry Frohock on Flo Porter's phone. He answered on the first ring.

"Have you got anything for me?" I asked.

"Jeeter, Baby, you better tread lightly on this one. I got nothing definite but there could be some very mean customers involved. Did you ever hear of Salvatore Pancione?"

"He has a sand and gravel business somewhere I think."

"That's one of the brothers. Or sons, maybe. There's a whole tribe of Pancione brothers, uncles, nephews - you name it. Sal lives in style on the South Shore. Nobody gets in to see him. Nobody's ever been able to pin anything on him. Nobody talks about him above a whisper. I don't even like you should know it's me saying this. I deny it already. But there's a kinda rumor in the wind Sal's ready to branch out. What's more, someone they call The Senator is supposed to be in this with him."

I'd heard of The Senator. He was a former member of the state legislature who had dreamed of going to Washington but he got caught taking bribes and was forced to resign. It was a big stink that somehow blew away without prosecution. Selwin Rose was the man's name. He lived in Falmouth. Long years in Boston and Massachusetts politics had given him knowledge of pressure points, those sensitive buttons one can touch, just so, to open doors.

"You still with me, Jeeter?"

"I'm just wondering how you get to know so many things, Jerry."

"Don't ask."

"Knowing who the enemy is is half the battle sometimes. I'll never be able to repay you for this one."

"Don't fret, Kiddo. Knowing you're the opposition changes the odds. I know that. No one else does. That's worth money. But take care. These guys make their own rules. And they both especially don't like jigaboos."

"That just adds zest to the contest, Uncle."

"Keep me posted, Son."

"I'll do that, Fatha."

37

Saturday night in a small Cape Cod town did not promise to be very lively. Maybe a few restaurants and taverns down the road would be noisy.

Tom Porter went to bed early. He'd eaten out and came in loaded. By ten o'clock he was snoring. He'd never know it even if his own bed was burning.

I prowled outdoors, dressed in dark clothes. The lights went out in Huck's house by eleven. Flo turned in before midnight. There hadn't been any sign of Seelye ever since he'd told me to get lost and then had driven away.

The sky was clear and full of stars so the day's heat radiated away quickly. I found my feet getting wet because dew was forming on the grass. A knitted hat and sweater felt good when I put them on. The tide was out and the special pungent hydrogen sulfide reek of marsh rot, organic matter recycling, filled my nostrils - a sweet unpleasantness.

By one o'clock only an occasional car whirred by on the main road. In the big silence I heard an owl call repeatedly from a grove of trees beyond Huck's barn.

I walked to keep warm; later, just to stay awake. The tide came back in. By the dock, each time I checked that spot, black water was higher, lapping at the pilings. I heard a fish break somewhere in the creek, the smash that a good bass makes once in a while. And along the road, in the black locusts, katydids, as the night wore on, sounded their rasping triplets with less and less insistence.

Once, a car stopped near Huck's driveway. I saw four young guys get out and take a leak and then jump back into a

Dodge that took off burning rubber. A town cruiser came by half a dozen times, slowed down, but didn't stop.

Nothing suspicious happened. The note had said three days. Maybe things would be quiet until Monday, but I couldn't count on that.

The sky paled and the stars vanished. Catbirds and robins began calling. When the sun came up I went into the house and fixed toast with jam and found some orange juice.

I was eating when Flo entered the kitchen. She had on a long blue wrapper but her feet were bare.

"Were you up all night?" she asked.

I told her everything had been quiet except for an owl on Huck's place.

"That's a great horned owl," she said. "A pair has nested there for several years now. It's early for them to be calling, though. Do you want some coffee?"

"No thanks," I said. "I'm going to get a few hours sleep after I finish this."

She perked some real coffee in a battered pot. Its aroma filled the kitchen.

We were the only ones awake in the house. She was probably naked under the faded robe. She had to know that I would speculate on that, yet she moved without self-consciousness - a radiantly healthy vital woman in her mid-thirties with needs not being met and potentials being wasted.

- The fatuous male, I said to myself. God's gift to the deprived and unsatisfied women of the world. Wise up, Dummy. She may be a prize. You aren't.

"Did you learn anything with that phone call last evening?" she asked.

"I'm not sure," I said.

"You don't want to talk about it?"

"I may drive to Falmouth later on. I have a possible lead."

The percolator was bubbling and the smell of coffee was something I could almost taste just by inhaling.

"Can you give me a name?"

Our eyes met. "Selwin Rose," I said.

"I've heard that name somewhere."

"He was a state rep for Norfolk county a few years back. Got caught collecting pay-offs. Resigned his office and was never called to account. He's also known as The Senator."

"And someone you phoned told you he might be in back of this attempt to make us sell our land."

"Mrs. Porter..."

"Please call me Flo."

"Flo..." It didn't come naturally to call her by her first name. "Flo, it would be better if you forgot that I made that call. Someone might request the number I dialed and get to my source. That could hurt a lot of people."

She poured an inch of black coffee into a cup and brought it to her lips to taste it. "Don't you want a sip?" she asked then, holding the cup out to me.

I took the cup from her hand and had a swallow. It was too hot to drink but it was the real thing. No instant substitute came close. I handed the cup back to her. "Thanks," I said.

"You seem to have a lot of respect for these people, who-ever they are, that we're up against."

"It's a sound idea to assume that the enemy is formidable, always."

"Will we be able to hold out against them?"

"They may make it hard to do so. Tell me, is there any-place you could go where no one could follow?"

"You still think I'm the weak link."

"On the contrary. I think you're the one who won't break and they'll have to break you to get what they want."

"I'm not going to run away."

"In that case I'll have to stay close to you."

She was holding the cup in both hands, breathing the steam still rising from it. "All right," she said.

$\mathcal{W}$e got into my car together at nine-thirty. She was wearing a hand-knitted open-necked sweater over a pale yellow cotton dress. A small purse hung from her left shoulder. Her shoes looked Italian and she looked wonderful. I'd put on a dark suit and tie, a white shirt with a button-down collar. We could have been a Sunday couple going off to church - except for the difference in color.

I took route 28 to Falmouth and wasted a few minutes in wrong turns before locating The Senator's home in Quissett. He owned one of those big old Victorian houses with all kinds of plantings, a wide porch, three floors, crenellations, a circular tower.

After two rings the door was opened by a black man in a suit that could have been a chauffeur's uniform. Maybe he was driver and valet both. He could have been a bodyguard as well. His eyes lingered on me but Flo rated only a glance. "Yes?" he said.

"We've come about a donation of the Pentecostal Shrine. The Senator should be expecting us," I said.

"I kinda doubt it," the man said. "This is Sunday, you know."

"I'm aware of that," I said. "In fact, that's why we're here. This concerns a rather large donation."

"To, or from, the Shrine?"

This guy was about as easy to con as a matron in a women's prison.

"I believe the matter should be discussed with the Senator in person," I said. "Would you please let him know that we are here?"

The man hesitated. He sensed something discordant but he couldn't identify it. "Wait here," he ordered, and closed the door in our faces.

It was a long wait, but when the door opened again it was The Senator who stood there. "Good morning," he said, studying both of us. "What can I do for you?"

He had all of the look of a big city politician. He was tall, stood straight, had a full head of white wavy hair and a pink close-shaven face. Maybe he thought we were a pair of Jehovah's Witnesses. If we'd had a silent child with us he could have been certain.

"We understand you are looking for a donation to your campaign," I said.

He smiled. "Won't you please come in."

He led us through a spacious entrance hall into a room with a fireplace and three sofas and lots of chairs, more a meeting room than a livingroom. The furnishings were ornate, heavy and ill-assorted. It was a place where overweight cigar-smoking men, drink in hand, might gather to discuss plans and strategies.

"I'm afraid I didn't catch your names," The Senator said.

"That's because we haven't thrown them at you yet, Mr. Rose."

He stiffened. He'd been on the point of asking us if we'd like to sit down. Now he changed his mind. "Perhaps I shouldn't have asked you in," he said.

"You're probably right, but here we are."

"So who are you?" He'd raised his voice and the black chauffeur had appeared in the doorway."

"Better run along and polish the car," I said to him. "We're going to be talking business."

"Shall I put him out, Boss?"

Rose was giving Flo the once over. I didn't like the look on his face. "Let's find out what he wants first," he said. "What do you want?" he said, turning to me.

"You're the one who wants something," I said. "A certain parcel of land, being ninety acres more or less."

His expression changed. "I have no idea what you're talking about," he said.

But he did. I could tell. He must have been a lousy poker player.

"Oh yes you do, Rose. And what's more, you are going to get on the phone as soon as we leave and you are going to call Sal Pancione, or some flunky of his, and tell him that we know who wants to get their cruddy fingers on the ninety acres. And you better make clear that any further attempts at coercion will be reported to federal authorities."

Rose let his eyes slip past me to his handyman. With his head he signaled Out.

"Save your face for another time," I said. "I don't like to mess up a brother."

He didn't get the message."

He was heavier and taller and younger than I and he had the cocky walk of an unbeaten light-heavyweight. He came at me, arms away from his sides, hands opened. Maybe he

43

thought he was going to pick me up like a baby and heave me through the door.

I always keep some small change in my left pants pocket. It was in my hand by then. I flipped a dozen pennies and dimes at his face. He raised his hands to ward them off as I stepped inside and delivered a vicious open-handed blow far below the belt. He folded forward toward me as I stepped back and chopped down on his right collarbone. A thick muscle there almost protected him, but it wasn't flexed at that moment and I felt the collarbone snap.

He teetered in front of us, tears of pain in his eyes, his right arm useless and his left hand still clutching his genitals.

"You can keep the change," I said.

Flo and I walked out. The Senator hadn't said another word.

She was quiet in the car for a long time. She'd glance my way and then look back into herself again.

"Physical violence is ugly," she said at last, speaking more to herself than to me. "I've watched you hurt two men now and I need to know what my feelings are.

"There's immediate revulsion at the sight of injury to a healthy body and some of that is due to the inability to watch without sharing in pain inflicted. That's an emotional response. There's also a dispassionate, non-partisan, post facto reaction: What you did was necessary and effective, therefore laudable. There's something else, though, something deeper, and it disturbs me."

"What is it?" I asked.

She had trouble saying it but was too much a scientist not to get it out. "It was exciting, too," she said softly.

I held my right hand out toward her, palm up, and she took it in both of hers. Hands can be joined in ways as intimate as the coupling of two bodies. The interlocking of our fingers was an understanding on several levels.

"You welcome the challenge, don't you," she said. The fingers of her right hand were learning the knars and creases and calluses of mine.

"Civilization has spread a very thin veneer over most of our most primitive urges," I said, not too sure to what urgings I was referring at the moment. "The primitive part of me lives close to the surface. When someone gets in my way I enjoy moving him aside."

"You provoke people though, don't you?"

"It's my way of finding out who they are."

"And establishing a pecking order."

I hadn't thought of it that way but I saw that she was right.

"I'm a throwback," I said, half in jest. "I want to know who's the dominant male in the wolf pack - or the pack of dogs."

"And you like it," she said. We were moving slowly through Falmouth traffic. "You like it the way the females stand watching, with their tongues hanging out, to see who will be the victor."

Was she likening herself to a bitch that had stood there with her tongue hanging out while I turned The Senator's lacky into a whimpering pup? She knew how to take things apart and find out how they worked. It was a sign of special clear headedness that she could examine her own feelings with the same impartiality.

A van came out of a side street and cut in front of us. I needed both hands for driving.

"You mentioned a name - Sal Something," she said. "Is he the one really behind all our trouble?"

"He and Rose seem to be in it together. Rose didn't know who we were until I mentioned the ninety acres. Then he gave himself away. We know he's part of it now. And since that half of the rumor has been confirmed there's not much doubt that Salvatore Pancione is the money and the motivating force behind it."

"But who is Salvatore Pancione?"

"The newspapers always refer to him as a 'reputed crime boss.' Actually, not much is known about him. There *is* such a person but almost no one has ever seen him. Maybe he's a figurehead but I doubt it. He's part of, or head of, a very formidable organization."

"Will Rose tell him we know he's behind this?"

"I'm sure he'll send word. I doubt if he can contact Sal directly."

"Will this Sal be scared off?"

"That's the big question. Sal would have preferred having his name kept out of it. So would Rose. Now, if they order any more attempts to force a sale, they may find the FBI moving in on them. My guess is that The Senator will want out. But Pancione may have the opposite reaction."

"You haven't notified the FBI yet have you?"

"Not yet. They need more than rumors before they'll come in."

"So we just have to wait until something happens."

"Hoping that nothing will."

$\mathcal{W}$hen we got back to the house, Porter was in the driveway. His arm was in a loose sling, but not his tongue.

"Where the Hell have you been?" he demanded.

"We drove to Falmouth," Flo said, as we got out of the car.

"For an hour in a motel, I suppose?"

Flo wasn't going to dignify his question with an answer but he insisted.

"I asked you if you went to a motel," he said.

"Is that what you expect?" she replied.

He turned on me. "I told you we didn't need you. We fired you. Now I want you to get off my property and stay away."

"Mr. Porter," I said, "we've just finished seeing a man in Quissett named Selwyn Rose. We've found out that he is one of the ones trying to make you sell out. The man behind Rose is a very powerful figure in organized crime. I would enjoy watching those two vultures pick you clean. They could do it, too. But your wife and Frank Huck have asked me to stay on here. So get used to it. I'm staying."

"I'll have you arrested for trespassing."

"You'll get yourself arrested for irrational behavior. Now go someplace and suck your thumb."

His left hand had been in the pocket of the Safari jacket he was wearing. He pulled it out now and there was a small calibre pistol in it. It didn't look like an American product.

47

"I'll kill you, you fucking dinge," he said, and he raised his arm to point the weapon at my head. He was shaking all over. Even at three paces he probably would have missed.

I didn't move. I saw tears welling up in his eyes. Love and murder are often the children of the same parent. He still wanted his wife's esteem and I'd shamed him before her. He wanted to kill both of us, but he couldn't pull the trigger.

"Let me have the gun," I said, and slowly extended my hand.

For a split second I feared that the sound of my voice had given him the courage he needed. Then he sagged, like a potted plant needing water, and I took the gun from his hand. He turned and went stumbling back toward the house.

I glanced at Flo. She was watching her husband retreat. "He wasn't always so pathetic," she said. "There was a time when he almost made it to the top in sports."

Was she afraid I'd think less of her for marrying him, or was she remembering better days when they had loved each other and he'd been a man in her eyes?

"Do you know how to use this?" I asked, indicating the pistol.

She turned back to me. "I tried it out a few years ago," she said. "Tom got it because a prowler was seen in the neighborhood. Then he wanted me to know how to handle it too. I guess I could still fire it if I had to."

"Then why don't you keep it," I said. "It's loaded. It's been kept in good shape. If we have callers one of these days, this could make a difference for you."

She put it in her purse. She was looking into herself again. There was an expression she had when that was going on. Her eyes focused on a vague middle distance and her mouth went slack. She followed her husband into the house and didn't look back at me.

Sometime after two AM I heard them. A cruiser had gone by slowly a few minutes earlier. Maybe they'd walked in from a mile away. They didn't drive up in a car.

I was in the shadows in the grove from which the owl had called the night before. There was a crunch of gravel on the driveway. You'd think any novice would have known better than to make a sound like that.

The one in the drive was only an outline against the star-glow of the sky. His partner was a dim form on the grass ten paces behind him moving more cautiously. Both were headed toward Huck's barn and each seemed to be carrying something, containers of some sort. They were the arsonists.

I let them reach the barn. When they went inside I ran across the open space between and crouched behind the barn door which they'd left half open.

The horse stomped and I heard a gurgle as the contents of a container were emptied. The smell reached me at the same time. It was gasoline. One of the men backed out the door dribbling the last of the gas from a one gallon jug.

I had my gun in my hand. As he came even with me I swung the gun at the back of his head. He never suspected a thing. He pitched forward and lay with his face in the wet trail he had just made. He was out cold.

The other man must have heard the sound and seen his partner fall forward. There was the crash of what sounded like a .45 and pieces of the barn door struck me in the face. I don't know where the bullet went. At the same instant, the whole inside of the barn exploded into flames. I was knocked over backwards but wasn't hurt. The horse was screaming.

The second man came through the door. His pants legs were aflame. I raised my arm from where I was lying and put a shot through the upper part of his right leg. He'd lost his own gun when the barn exploded. His screams joined those of the horse as he want down.

I got to my feet. Huck came running, pulling the two hoses we'd hooked up in advance.

"Take this one," he said, "and keep it on me."

I spun the nozzle and turned the jet of water on Huck while he went into the flames. For an agonizing minute he disappeared. Then he came into view again, leading the horse.

I heard sirens in the distance. Flo had been wakened when the barn went up and had phoned for help, she told me later.

I saw that Huck was singed and he was coughing painfully but the screen of water had protected him fairly well.

The horse was terrified. It was all Huck could do to keep him from bolting. He led the poor animal around to the other side of his home, out of sight of the burning barn.

I turned the hose on the man I'd shot. He was still screaming in pain. The burns on his legs would be a long time healing. The bullet in his upper leg had smashed the femur. He was still conscious. He was going to live.

Lying at the gate of Inferno was the other man. I soaked him and then dragged his inert body away from the barn. It was too late. He'd inhaled gasoline fumes and they'd ignited in his lungs.

The volunteer fire department did its best. Some of the barn was saved. Most of the equipment too.

A rescue squad took the injured man to the Cape Cod Hospital. I asked a cop to travel with him. Then I got in my own car and drove down the main road to see if I could locate whatever transportation the two arsonists had used

I'd waited too long. If there had been a getaway car, and a driver, it was gone. So was the chance to trace a vehicle.

By the time I got back to Huck's place, everyone had left except Huck and Flo. Porter had slept through the whole thing. Seelye hadn't been around since he'd told me to get lost.

"The police weren't happy to see you disappear," Huck said.

"I'll go to the station and make a full report in a few hours," I said. Are you all right? Any bad burns?"

"Lost a little hair, but that's about all."

He'd lost more than a little and I saw some raw places on his hands.

"What about you?" Flo asked.

We were standing by one of the lights in the driveway. "You've got something wrong with the side of your face."

I touched it. "Must be pieces of the barn door," I said.

Flo stepped closer. "Let's go back to the house where I can see what you need."

We went to her wing of the house and she sat me on the closed toilet in her bathroom while she and Huck looked for splinters in my cheek and the left side of my neck.

Flo used tweezers and alcohol. "These are not easy to see," she said.

"That's one of the advantages of being white," Huck said. "You get a face full of splinters, they're easy to see."

"A white face in the night is an easy target," I said. "I'd rather catch a few splinters than a bullet."

51

"You must have come close to catching both. The cops found the gun in the barn when the fire was out. It was an old Army .45. It blew one Hell of a hole in the door."

Flo's hands were quick and sure. There was blood all over my dark sweater before she was through. Some of the wood fragments had been in pretty deep. She took the sweater and said she'd wash it. She lathered the area she'd worked on and wiped it gently and put a couple of bandaids on the worst spots. "We better watch you for a couple of days," she said. "There could be some infection. Have you had a tetanus booster lately?"

"Less than a year ago," I said. "A whole wall fell on me that time."

"Should we ask what happened then?"

"Someone aimed a car at me. I dodged behind a brick wall. The car came half way through it."

"Tell me," Huck asked. "Whatever do you do for excitement?"

"He plays checkers," Flo said.

I looked at her. How had she known a thing like that? Was she clairvoyant?

"It just popped out," she said, as if I'd asked her out loud.

"Is that true?" Huck asked.

I was shaking my head in disbelief. "All my life I've loved playing checkers," I said. "It's a much more complex game than most people imagine. But there's no way you could have known that about me."

"We know lots of things about other people," Flo said, "only we don't know we know them and we don't know how it happens."

"It's part of that primitive core we spoke of earlier, isn't it?" I said.

Huck was watching both of us. Momentarily, he'd become an outsider in the small bathroom.

"If you can brush away the words," Flo said, "if you can get underneath the tags and labels, there's an awareness there of signals to which we used to respond."

In the quiet that followed I was aware of other signals. These were two very fine people. I was their employee. They would pay me off when the job was done, if none of us got killed, and I'd be on the loose again.

But we were two men and one woman, also, and to the already strained, inchoate relationship between Flo and Huck were added my own intense feelings for this woman who responded instantly to what was elemental in me.

The cramped room was suddenly much too small. I stood up. "I'll go upstairs," I said, "and shower and sleep an hour. Thanks for patching me up."

I left them and climbed to my room and stepped onto the deck. The first pale steely light of day was rising into the sky above the marsh. A fresh clean smell of morning was on the land. Five ducks rocketed past, obeying signals only they could understand, and somewhere in the reeds a small bird let out a high whinnying cry.

When the Chief had my complete report on tape, I asked about the .45 that had been fired at me and that had set off the conflagration.

"It's an Army .45 from World War II," he said. "Thousands of them never got turned in at the end of the war. There's no hope of a trace on it."

"What about the men?" I asked. "Any names?"

"They weren't carrying identification and the one in the hospital isn't talking. We've got their prints, though. There'll be a report before long. I'll let you know."

Something was bugging me. I didn't know if I should ask or not. "I'd like some time alone with the man in the hospital," I said anyway. "Is that all right with you?"

He didn't answer right away. When he did he said, "Remember, criminals are privileged persons these days. They have more rights than you do. More than I do, too. No rough stuff. The guy could probably initiate a criminal suit against you for firing on an unarmed man."

"Didn't he have a weapon on him?"

"He'll claim we planted it."

"I won't touch him, Chief. But I'll wager I can open him up."

"Maybe you can. Go ahead and try. Something else, Jeeter."

"What's that?"

"There's a man named Flavin. Black. Works for a former legislator from Quissett. Flavin was admitted to the Falmouth Hospital yesterday - broken collarbone and ruptured left testicle. A little birdie told me you had been to pay him a social call. Putting people in hospitals all over the Cape is not gonna make you very popular. What about that episode?"

I should have told him sooner.

"Flavin's employer," I said, "Selwyn Rose, also known as The Senator, is one of the men behind the attempt to gain control of the ninety acres owned by the Porters and Seelye and Huck."

"How did you find that out?"

"Chief, I have my sources. You have yours. Neither will be any good again if they get revealed."

He didn't like it but he couldn't refute it.

"So you paid him a Sunday morning visit. With Mrs. Porter."

How did he get that information?

"I did."

"And what did you learn?"

"I confirmed the rumor. Rose is part of the scheme."

"And when he understood that you had his number he asked his bouncer to teach you a lesson."

"Right."

"Did you know that Flavin was in the ring for about six years and fought some of the best of them?"

"I didn't know his name then, but I had the feeling he'd been a fighter."

"You suckered him."

"At one thirty-eight I wasn't going to go toe to toe with a pro who weighs close to one seventy."

"Flavin is gonna want to see you dead. When he comes after you he'll only get close enough to shoot."

"So I'll have to shoot first."

"Jeeter, I hope it happens in some other township. I don't want any more bodies in my town."

*A*t the hospital I didn't ask any questions. The Chief had given me the room number so I just strolled in. If you ask permission in big institutions you get a run around and a hundred rules and regulations are thrown at you, but if you simply walk through, everyone thinks you belong. Maybe with my pock-marked bandaged face I looked like an ambulatory patient.

The cop in the room remembered me. He was glad to go out for air when I suggested he take a break.

I pulled a chair up next to the man in the bed. His eyes were bloodshot. He needed a shave. A scar from his left eyebrow to the corner of his mouth had long ago given his face a twisted look.

"How you doin'?" I asked.

"Who wants to know?"

"Your mother sent me to make sure you're comfy."

"Fuck you, nigger. I seen you somewhere."

"That's right. You owe all your good luck to me."

He squinted. "You're the one that plugged me, aren't you? Sure. You shot me, you bastard."

"Just being a good citizen. You know how it is. I could have let you burn to death, too. But I put out the flames. Don't I get some thanks for that?"

"You shit-faced cock-sucker, I'll kill you." If he'd been able to move, he might have tried.

"Well," I said, "now that we've dispensed with the pleasantries, let's get down to business. What's your name?"

"Go to Hell."

"Look," I said, "we got your prints last night. You're the kind has a record going back to when you were a juvenile. We'll have that record and your name in only a few more hours. You're in big trouble. The law and the courts might only put you away for a short while for arson, or attempted arson, or trespassing, or whatever trivial offense it winds up as. But the people who hired you are gonna put you away for good."

"That's what you say."

"It's true and you know it. You got caught. Even if you don't tell us anything, your record is going to lead us to who hired you. Your buddy is dead, you know. But we have his prints too."

"I want a lawyer."

"Why not? He'll get you out on bail and the next day you'll be dead. Is there anyone who'll care?"

"You're full of shit."

"It happens from time to time. But I'm gonna be walking around for a while yet and you aren't. Maybe you don't even know what this is all about. Do you?"

"I don't know nothin'."

I let him see that I didn't doubt that.

"Then allow me to elucidate," I said. "We're pretty sure that Salvatore Pancione wants to set up a little Vegas on the land where you tried to burn down a barn. You ever heard of Sal?"

"Never heard of him."

"Yeah. That's about as likely as dogs don't get ticks."

"What?"

"Never mind. So Sal doesn't know yet that we're on to him. But if I go from you to him and tell him we know his game, who do you think he's gonna decide tipped me off?"

Those blood-shot eyes were almost closed and the guy's teeth were clamped together and grinding. He didn't know I'd been to see The Senator and had already tipped off all concerned.

"Are you beginning to understand," I asked, "how little time you may have left?"

"What's in it for me if I talk?"

"We can get you transferred out of here into another hospital under a name that will look legitimate. You'll at least live long enough to heal and to stand trial."

"Some deal. Anyway, I think you're lyin'."

"All I want is the name of who hired you and where to find him."

"You're wastin' your time."

He was ready to start making those those routine I'm-tougher-than-you type protests that so often precede capitulation. Another ten minutes and he'd be giving me what I wanted.

A nurse came in with a tray in her hand. "Time for your antibiotics," she said.

She was heavy-set, about forty years old, no shape at all. Burly. She lifted a hypodermic from the tray, raised the sheet off the patient's thigh, squeezed a drop of pale liquid into the air and then jabbed the needle into a red hairy buttock.

She pulled the sheet back into place and then left without looking at me or the man on the bed.

When the door closed again I turned back to the injured man.

He had his mouth open and his color had changed. He was turning blue. The blood-shot eyes were bulging and his body was rigid. He couldn't breathe.

I lunged for the door and got into the hall. The heavy-set nurse had vanished but a closed door to my right was marked Stairway.

Why had I sent away the cop?

An MD with a clipboard in hand was staring at me.

"In there," I shouted, pointing. "The patient was just given an injection that paralyzed the central nervous system. He'll be dead in minutes if you can't do something for him."

I yanked open the door to the stairway and as I started down I heard a clatter two floors below. At the ground floor level I found a heap of clothes - a nurse's uniform, a cap and a wig. Was I chasing a man or a woman?

The door opened onto a parking lot. For a second I lost my bearings. Then I saw my own car and I heard a motor start up. A dark green Mazda GLC headed for the exit burning rubber. Behind me people were shouting.

I ran for my car, got in and took off after the Mazda. A cop almost got in my way. It wasn't the cop I had sent out for a breather.

The Mazda went down Camp Street and got into clogged traffic at the light by the railroad crossing. I was five cars behind and couldn't get any closer but I couldn't take a chance on getting out and running.

The driver of the Mazda had a gray pork-pie hat on and at this distance didn't look anything like the nurse I'd watched in the hospital, but I really hadn't looked when I should have. Any kind of uniform gives the wearer anonymity - cop, soldier, usher - you don't look at the face because you've got a label already. Hadn't Flo said something in that connection earlier?

I saw the Mazda turn left on Iyanough Road and followed, blowing my horn and doing my best to attract attention, passing, any chance I got, and cutting into the right lane and up on business property when I could gain a length that way.

I had my gun out on the seat beside me and there were only two cars between us when a grotesque fat female pushing a shopping cart stepped into my path. It probably would have wrecked my car if I'd hit her. I spun the wheel and missed her by inches but three more cars got in front of me. I was back to where I started.

At the Airport Rotary the Mazda headed for the 132 exit. I got into the right lane but at the last moment the other driver veered left and shot around the rotary so he/she was only a couple of cars behind me. As I passed the 132 turn off he went that way and I had to circle the rotary another time before resuming pursuit.

We tore past the fast food drive-ins and the mall and the motels. When we got beyond the light at Bearse's Way, on that long downhill straightaway, there were traffic lines in both directions. We were passing on the right most of the time and I was gaining but on the sandy shoulders it was a miracle we both didn't lose control.

Only three cars separated us as we approached the Mid-Cape Highway and again I got fooled. The guy (or woman) got into the right lane as if to go through to route 6-A, or even to loop around onto the Mid-Cape. He slowed down and I was right behind him then. A truck was coming up behind me on my left. Without warning, the guy cut in front of the truck, skidded into a left turn, and sped through the parking lot and past the service station.

I was cut off by the truck and by the time I could turn, I had to go through the back side of the parking lot and the Mazda was already half way up the hill by the water tower.

Sirens were wailing behind me. I made out a State Police car in the rear view mirror overtaking me fast. At the top of the hill I pulled into the Rest Area and jumped out. I left my gun on the seat and produced my license as the cruiser came alongside.

Luckily, the cop was not one of the self-important ones. He was young and sharp.

"Can you radio ahead to set up a block on the green Mazda?" I asked, as I handed him my private investigator's license.

"I already did," he said. He took a quick look at my ticket. "Get in," he said, and we took off with the siren screaming and the lights flashing.

He was on the radio, driving one-handed. We were doing over eighty. He told someone to stand by my car. "Slate-blue Tercel," he was saying. "Driver is now with me."

"And my gun is on the front seat of the Tercel," I told him.

"Says his gun is on the front seat. See that nobody touches it."

A mile ahead, I could see lights flashing all across the road. Traffic was slowing. We drove onto the median strip to get closer. The Mazda was in the sand at the side of the highway and as we pulled near, the driver got out, hands over her head, two shotguns aimed at her.

The pork-pie hat had fallen off revealing short black hair. She was wearing a pale pink sweater and a mini-skirt. The white shoes and white cotton stockings were unchanged.

If she'd gotten into her car and only sat there with the hat on I probably never would have known who to follow. Cars come and go by he hospital all the time, day and night. Only precipitous flight had been her undoing.

*A*n hour later, the Chief and I and a lieutenant from the State Police, named Talbot, were all closeted in the lieutenant's office in south Yarmouth. Slowly, my story had been checked and rechecked and Talbot had almost decided to accept it. He was not one of the quick ones.

A phone call to the hospital had confirmed the death of the man I had talked to there. Asphyxiation as a result of a massive injection of curare was the apparent cause of death. The alleged murderess was being held in a cell at the barracks for the moment.

"So you sat there and watched a murder committed and didn't do a thing." The lieutenant was determined to label me a fool. I wondered how many blacks were under him - and how they fared.

"Lieutenant..."

"And the night before, you fractured a man's skull and subsequently he died."

"That man died in a fire he was going to ignite."

"You also drove your own car through heavy traffic at speeds more than double some of the posted limits, crossing center lanes, passing on the right, endangering pedestrians and other motor vehicle operators in the most flagrant manner possible."

I'd had about enough of him.

"So why don't you lock me up," I said, "and turn loose the woman who committed the murder and see if you can get yourself an award for valor?"

"I don't like wise apples, Mister."

"And I don't like dumb cops," I said, as I stood up to go.

The Chief was on his feet too.

"Lieutenant," he said, "this man hasn't slept more than a couple of hours in more than two days and he's been through a lot in that time, including some injuries. So he's a little bit tense right now. Make some allowances. We've got a situation building that could hurt the Cape the worst way possible. Jeeter has found out more in one week-end about what we're up against than you and I could have uncovered in a month."

"Speak for yourself, Chief."

"All right. He's found out more than I could have in a long long time. Maybe you have more resources. People who order arson twice and a murder all in one week are not the kind we want on this side of the Canal. Chances are that with that phony nurse in custody - thanks to Jeeter - we can tie her to the big man on the South Shore and block his plans."

The lieutenant was still seated. He was slow to move. "Something you maybe forget," he said, "is that Mr. Pancione has a bundle of clout. We don't annoy people like that on hearsay."

"I'll keep that in mind," the Chief said. "Now, with your permission, I'll drive Jeeter to where his car is parked and we'll all get back to work."

We walked out. The Chief didn't say a word until he'd driven more than a mile down the road. Then he said, "Jeeter, someday you've got to learn how to eat humble pie."

"That's a polite way of saying I should suck ass, Chief. I must be a retarded type. That, I'll never learn."

"Another minute and that big bozo would have put you in a cell."

"How long could he have kept me there?"

The Chief took his eyes off the road to look at me. "You sure do push people pretty hard," he said.

"I'd like to shove that dumb pencil-pusher some more," I said. "He's on the take. I'd bet my last buck on it. He doesn't care if an army of gamblers takes over down here. People like you will be long gone. You said it yourself. And people like him will be in clover, pocketing top salaries from an embattled citizenry as their righteous and stalwart defender, meanwhile

63

accepting every kind of pay-off from hoodlums and thieves for winking and looking the other way. He's a bigot, too."

"Is that what riles you the most?"

"No, it isn't. I've learned to live with prejudice. Even when it's so well disguised the person has fooled himself, there's always that whisper of condescension, that bit of excessive heartiness that gives him away. If a dozen times a year I meet a white man, or woman, who looks at me and doesn't see my black face first, it's a miracle. So I don't let it bother me. Not enough to matter. Not enough to prejudice me.

"What bothers me about that beefy lieutenant is his betrayal of trust. He's not interested in wiping out crime. He'd be out of a job if there were no more criminals on the loose. He's the sort who glories in an occasional drug bust - some kids getting high on pot, or a crackdown on speeders. Can't you just hear him? 'We have had enough of the wanton slaughter that occurs annually on our highways.' But any operation that can be counted on to function on a large scale, outside the law, that's something that establishes his role as intermediary. That's the big threat that makes his job a necessity. There are hundreds and hundreds of decent people in every sector of law enforcement. The few crooks and phonies negate the work of thousands."

"When you start climbing the ladder, Jeeter, you have to make concessions. I have to pretend to agree with lots of people, often, when I don't want to."

"You don't need to explain that sort of thing to me, Chief. Everyone has to look to see what's best for himself and often you have to fudge a little to make sure not to alienate support. But I know you're not the kind to try to keep on the good side of someone like Pancione. You aren't for sale. You've accepted the trust of those who made you Chief. That stuffed sausage back at the barracks doesn't know the meaning of the word."

64

We'd reached the Rest Area. My car was where I'd left it. We pulled in behind it.

"How can I get to talk with that pseudo nurse?"I asked.

"I'll try to arrange it," the Chief said, "but Talbot is going to say No."

"They can't keep her at the barracks very long."

"A preliminary hearing should take place at the Courthouse. Maybe the DA will let you have a conference."

"You know, she's in the same boat her victim was a few hours ago. It didn't take long to get to him."

The Chief revved the motor. I got out and shut the door and leaned back into the window. "Demotion is quick and sorta final in this league. We need a living link to Pancione, Chief. Someone who'll testify."

"Did you get anything from the man in the hospital before he got...demoted?"

"Another ten minutes and he was going to give me a name. That's when the nurse came in."

"Maybe people live longer if you stay away from them, Jeeter."

What could I answer? There seemed to be some truth in that.

The Chief took off and I got into my car. My gun wasn't there anymore.

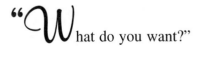 "What do you want?"

Seelye had come to the door himself. He was clean-shaven - that is if flaring sideburns allowed the term. Funny how I hadn't noticed before how they gave him a look of belonging to an earlier time. He was wearing another three-piece suit but he had slippers on. Perhaps he was about to go out.

"I thought it was time for just you and me to have a talk," I said.

"I have no wish to talk with you."

"That doesn't surprise me, Mr. Seelye. In fact, that's one reason why I decided to come here."

"I thought I'd made it clear enough so that even someone like you might understand that I have no further need of you. You've been fired. Now please be so kind as to go away."

He started to close the door in my face. I put my hand against it. I took the door jamb in my left hand for leverage and forced the door wide open.

"I don't get turned away easily," I said, and stepped inside. "Even someone like you can eventually manage to understand that." He had backed up. He was a good four inches taller than I and he wore a haughty patrician look of disdain. There'd been times when I'd let that kind of superior mien cow me. Not anymore.

"Now that you've asked me in," I said, "suppose you lead the way to a comfortable place to sit and talk."

I've got to hand it to him. He kept his cool. He showed me his back and walked through the hall into a room that contained a large desk and a number of easy chairs. Law books filled the wall behind the desk. French windows looked out on a flagstone patio. Wall-to-wall carpeting in a turquoise blue increased the light but lent an equivocal air to the apparently serious uses to which the room might be put.

Seelye sat behind the desk. I wondered if he kept a revolver in one of the drawers. Instead of sitting in front of the desk I pulled a chair to one side so that I could watch what he did with his hands. He sat perfectly still and stared at me, waiting for me to start.

I was in no hurry. I took in the heavy flowered drapes at the windows, the expensively framed reproductions on the walls, the fact that the armchairs were vinyl and not leather, which they were supposed to imitate.

The house was small, in a development that went back maybe ten years, every lot neatly landscaped. There were no longer any small children on the street, or very few. Seelye undoubtedly had a master bedroom and bath and guest room upstairs, with kitchen, family room, dining area and utility room at this level. There would be no basement. A carport at the end of the twenty-foot drive completed the layout.

It was not a rich man's home. It wasn't the home of a big shot lawyer. It was small time.

"You never married, did you?" I said at last.

He made me wait for an answer. "If you intend to probe my personal life, Mr. Jeeter, I'm afraid you'll learn nothing."

"Why didn't you marry?" I asked.

No answer.

"Well, not everybody finds it the best way of life. I can't imagine that a wife and little children would be your style anyway. Am I right?"

"I have some rather important things to do today," he said. "I hope you had something specific in mind when you forced your way in here."

"Not really," I said. "Just wanted to drop by, pay my respects, so to speak, to a former employer."

"In that case," he stood up, "you've done what you came to do so now..."

"Sit down," I said.

He gave me his best and snottiest down-his-long-nose look. "I am not accustomed to taking orders from members of the servant class," he said.

"Got a real hang-up there, haven't you?" I pointed an index finger at him. "Sit down, Seelye, or I'll have to get all the way out of this vinyl back-buster and make you sit down. And that would increase my impatience with you."

Like a child who pretends it was his idea anyway, he slowly returned to his seat.

"How long have you known Selwyn Rose?" I asked.

He didn't give himself away. Maybe I'd made a bad guess. "I don't think I even know the name," he said.

"He's also known as The Senator."

"Senators and former senators seem to like the Cape."

"This one never got to be senator. He was caught with his grubby fingers in the honey pot and retired early."

"So?"

"He's your type, Seelye."

"Perhaps you are deliberately trying to insult me. The effort strikes me as sophomoric." Caustic. I was supposed to crawl back into my hole.

"The thing is," I said, "Rose aspired to greater things but he was small time. He didn't make it. Isn't that about the story of your life too?"

He glanced at the watch on his wrist and then stared out the window at the rhododendrons in the patio. If I hadn't seen his foot twitching I wouldn't have known I'd touched a nerve.

"I think you want to sell out, Seelye. I think you and Rose know each other and are in this deal together. What you don't know is that the people into whose hands you are playing are big time. You're being used. You and Rose are less than servant class for these people. You're punks. Flunkies. When you've served their purpose you'll be dropped like soft turds and no one will want to pick you up, ever again."

I got to my feet. "Think it over, Counselor," I said. "Up to now you've still got that shack in the marsh where you can go and cry in your beer and bourbon and let your hair down. You go along with this deal and you'll wind up with nothing."

I left him sitting there. For a moment I even felt sorry for him. Maybe he could have done something with his life if he'd ever had a little backbone. It seemed as if fewer people all the time had any of that.

*T*he nurse's name was Paula S. Conway, maiden name - Fallon. She had been a nurse but was apprehended stealing electronic monitors and other costly hospital equipment at Peter Bent Brigham. The stolen goods were never recovered. It was thought that the Mob had set up a clinic somewhere, to take care of its own - a neat way of avoiding reports on injuries that could easily have led to arrest. A hood with a gunshot wound could be given an injection to knock him out, could then be transported in a closed vehicle to the clinic and he'd never know where he was. All personnel would wear surgical masks. The trip back home - or to a recovery area - would be under sedation in another closed vehicle.

Everything about the case pointed to a set-up of this sort, but Paula hadn't talked. She was the kind who never would. She did eighteen months at Framingham. Came out on probation and a year later disappeared. Where she'd been ever since, no one knew. Grand larceny was the only offense on her record. Until now.

I testified at the hearing in the First Court of Barnstable. Paula never spoke. She had a lawyer named Peltz, from Boston, who had appeared for a lot of other unsavory characters, too often with favorable results for the accused.

On the basis of my testimony, probable cause was found for holding her for trial for murder in the first degree. I got the feeling that probably cause for extreme caution was indicated in my regard. Without my eye witness account of the murder, the case would evaporate. There would be some disagreeable fellows gunning for me before long. Would they be after Paula too? Maybe not. Not if they got to me first.

I wasn't allowed to see Paula except in the courtroom where she appeared in handcuffs. She was as impassive as a block of stone. I think even the judge was impressed by the way she stood without moving while testimony was given. You wondered if any female attributes had ever been a part of her.

Her body looked like a single swollen mass of gristle. Her gray hair could have been uncarded steel wool. Thick eyebrows and an oversized beaked nose gave her face a shaded look, as if what was in the eyes and mouth had gone into hiding.

According to the record, she'd been born in Boston on June 9, 1946. Her last known address had been on East Brookline Street in the South End, but that was years ago. The original complaint against her was filed by an anesthesiologist named Kilpatrick, Stephen C. It was a starting place. Two of them, in fact.

$\mathcal{I}$ was worried about Flo Porter. I went back to the house and found her in the remains of Huck's barn. The horse was almost ready to accept his old stall again. Flo had been grooming him and talking to him. Huck was there.

"She's wonderful with that animal," he said. "I couldn't get him to come back in here. He spent the last two nights in the grove. Flo just talks to him and leads him around. After a while he followed her in here while I was getting things cleaned out. She didn't force him, just led the way."

"Frank said it was male pride that had been challenged." She tipped her head to one side as she said it and gave me a What-do-you-say look.

"You mean this horse said to himself - If a lowly female isn't afraid I can't be either?"

"Come on, I was only joking," Huck said.

"Horses are pretty smart creatures," I said, "but I don't honestly think they can talk to themselves."

Flo was shaking her head. "They can reason, though," she said. "At least they can make decisions based on accumulated data."

"What really happened," Huck was talking, "the horse accepted you as someone to be trusted. Your voice, manner, touch - he recognized a person who had his best interests at heart. He may have recognized some quality in you - maybe just femaleness - which you share with his former owner. Macho pride had nothing to do with it. Obviously."

So the ghost of Huck's wife had come into the barn too. Did she walk with him everywhere he went? There was something in Flo's face I couldn't put a tag on. Was it hurt? Was it compassion? She was a strong woman but for an instant a part of her had been stretched taut, almost to the breaking point.

There was an awkward silence, then I told them I had just come from the hearing and that I had a lead or two.

"So you'll be going up to Boston," Flo said.

"Somehow we've got to establish a connection between what's been happening here and the person or persons giving the orders."

"Will it take long? I mean, will you have to be gone long?" Huck asked.

"I don't know. I might get back by evening."

"Can I go with you?" It was Flo who had spoken - and I'd been on the point of asking if she'd come.

I looked at her and nodded. "That seems like a good idea. The more we all keep moving around, the more difficult it will be for someone to harm any of us."

I turned to Huck. "Keep it to yourself that we've taken off, will you. It'll give us a head start."

He said he would. He seemed to be trying to puzzle some-thing out. Maybe he'd sensed Flo's reaction to his remark about the horse and had understood it better than I. I thought he'd hurt her in some way. Perhaps he was just realizing what it meant if she could be hurt that easily.

We left him working on his barn and went to Flo's house. Tom Porter, as usual, was not at home. Flo disappeared for fifteen minutes and reappeared in a lavender dress with a yel-low sweater over it. She had on medium high-heeled shoes and carried a large purse over her shoulder. She'd taken time to shower so no lingering odor of horse came with her. She smelled of pine soap and sunlight and she was lovely to see.

We got into my little Toyota and drove to Boston. I parked in the Boston Common Garage and then we walked to Park Square where I rented a new Buick compact.

The next stop was East Brookline Street, in the shadow of the looming half-empty Cathedral Project. A vacant lot on the corner of St. George's Street had been turned into a vegetable garden.

It didn't take long to find the number where the nurse had once lived. There were three names beside the door and three bells. I rang all three in turn and got no answer from any of them.

We tried the next house. A young white woman with a baby in her arms opened the door enough to peak out. A heavy chair prevented it from opening any further.

"We're from the Department of Public Welfare," I said. "A lady named Paula S. Conway, who once lived next door, has a check due her but we can't seem to locate her. Have you ever heard her name?"

The young woman said she hadn't.

"Do you know who lives next door?"

"They're all students," she said.

"Does one of them own the building?"

"I think they bought it together as a sort of Coop. They just got it this year."

"You wouldn't know who the previous owner was, would you?"

"No. We only moved here three months ago ourselves."

I thanked her and we tried a half dozen other buildings but no one had ever heard of Paula Conway, or Paula Fallon.

We had the option of going to the Registry of Deeds and making a search for the owner of the building when Paula lived there - or had said she lived there. Or we could go looking for the anesthetist at Peter Bent. But I was betting that if Paula had actually lived here someone would remember her. In city neighborhoods there are always eyes watching. People don't often say what they've seen but someone always sees everything.

"Have you noticed anyone observing us?" I asked Flo.

"Across the way," she said. "There's a face at that window with the box of geraniums in it. Someone's been there ever since you rang the first bell. Looks like an elderly woman."

"Could you get her to open her window and talk to you?"

"I can try."

Flo crossed the street while I rang one more bell and a few minutes later called for me to join her. The window was up and I looked into the face of an old woman over the blooming geraniums. She had no teeth and the flesh of her cheeks had fallen in so that what stared out at me was all pits and hollows. Only the ears, pendulous and pink, and the nose, bulbous and veined, seemed intent on escaping the open craters around them.

"This is Mrs. Garabedian," Flo said. "She's lived her since 1953. She remembers Paula very well."

"If you really have a check for Paula, I hope you'll tear it up."

The voice was pitched low and seemed to resonate in the out-sized nose. The eyes were clear, though, and the way the lady looked at me I felt certain little escaped her.

"Was she known as Paula Conway when she lived here?" I asked.

"That's right. Mrs. Paula Conway."

"So there was a husband?"

"Sure was. A rough sort of man. Patrick Oh they called him. Maybe the Oh stood for a middle initial. Cars would pull

74

up in front of the house, someone leaning on the horn, someone else yelling 'Patrick Oh, are you comin?' They wouldn't go ring the bell like civilized people. Five minutes they'd be there yelling and honking. Then 'himself' would appear, pulling on a black leather jacket or stuffing his shirt in his pants, half the time his fly still unzipped."

"Do you know what he did for a living?"

She snorted. "He was one of them that lives at the track, at Suffolk Downs. She was the one that worked. A nurse. Worked regular too. Six days a week and long hours. For a man wasn't worth beans. A gambler and a hooligan. He got his, though."

"What do you mean?"

"I think he must have got in debt with his gambling. Probably borrowed from the sharks and then lost all he borrowed. I was right here when the usual car came for him one morning, horn blowing, someone yelling. But another car pulled up just down the street and two men got out and stood there, heads together, like they were talking quietly. Patrick Oh came out of his house and got to the sidewalk. He was just reaching for the car door when the car took off with a screech of rubber.

"That was when he noticed the other two men. They were walking toward him. He started to run back into his house but one of them tackled him. Then the two proceeded to beat him. One wrapped his leather belt around his right hand and hit Patrick Oh in the face until you couldn't tell it was a face at all. And when he collapsed they kicked him in the back where I guess the kidneys are. All the time, Paula was watching from the front window. They left him unconscious and went back to their car. When it drove away we saw that it had a piece of cardboard for a plate."

"Others watched, too. Is that right?"

"With the way Patrick Oh was screaming, must have been a dozen saw the whole thing."

"And no one raised a hand to stop it."

"You're no Social Worker, Sonny," she said, those sunken gimlet eyes on mine, "and you know no one interferes when a score is being settled."

Jungle justice, I knew. "When the car was gone. Did Paula come out of the house?"

"No sir. She may have called for an ambulance. One came and got her man. And the police came a little after and went ringing bells, like you've been doing, but nobody told them anything."

"How long ago did this happen? Do you remember?"

"It was in 1967. We never saw Patrick again. Maybe he died."

I doubted that. A beating, without a complaint, went in the files as a call to assist an injured man, injuries of unknown origin. Murder required an investigation. The pros were careful not to go that far. Conway had probably moved to another state after he got back on his feet. He would never have returned to any track in Massachusetts.

"But Paula went on living here after that, am I right?"

"She stayed on for about a year and a half but she changed. She still worked, only when she was off duty she'd wait till someone started down the street and she'd go after them and get them to give her five or ten dollars. 'I'll give it back before long,' she'd say, but no one ever saw anything back. We were almost all old people here then, most of us living on Social Security or a Welfare check. She was vicious when checks came. She was a muscular heavy woman and if you didn't give her what she asked for she'd hurt you one way or another. We didn't dare to complain."

"Do you think she was paying off the debts her husband had welched on?"

"That could be it. She had a desperate way at first, but later it seemed more like she enjoyed it, taking advantage of weak old people."

"Did anyone ever come to visit her?"

"Only men, but not many. And they didn't come for what you might be thinking. There were some that came nights, always two together, and they'd only stay for a couple of minutes. Different pairs each time, in different cars too. Then there was one man in his early forties who came the second Sunday of each month. He came alone and he'd stay about an hour each time. Sometimes he'd have a shopping bag with him and I think he'd leave off something with her. I never could find out what, though it may only have been groceries. He came on foot from somewhere in Southie and he had a stump where his right hand should have been. He always walked real slow. I used to wonder how many times he'd been robbed."

She was peering at me again. "Are you going to tell me why you're so interested in Paula?" she asked.

"You'll be safer not knowing."

"She's in trouble again, isn't she?"

"Was she in trouble before?"

"You know as well as I do, better I bet, that she was at Framingham for stealing things at the hospital where she worked."

"You've been very helpful, Mrs. Garabedian. I'm grateful to you."

"Come on, Sonny. Just about the only pleasure left me now is knowing what goes on."

"Do you have a phone, Mrs. Garabedian?"

"The man in the back room has one. He lets me use it if there's a real need."

"Will you promise to use it to call my answering service if anyone comes around asking about Paula or disturbing you in any way?"

"I will."

I gave her a card with my phone number on it. "Paula's being held without bail," I said, "for a murder I saw her commit. She won't be loose again for a long time. Maybe never."

*W*e walked back to the rental car and got in.

"It's amazing," Flo said. "A dozen people watched a man get beaten unconscious and no one did anything to stop it and afterwards no one would even admit they knew it happened."

"You've never lived in the city, have you?"

"I grew up in Amherst and went to school there and then moved to the Cape. Once in a while someone would be found dead from exposure. That's what they called it. It usually meant that a drunk passed out in a field and froze to death. I guess a house got broken into occasionally. Once I saw two students having a fist fight, but one shoved the other over on his tail and that was the end of it. No, I don't know much about violence."

"That old lady of the geraniums does. The first law of survival in the city is - Don't talk."

"Then why was she so willing to talk to us?"

"After eighteen years the rule breaks down. Also, she lives on gossip. She had us sized up as soon as she saw us. She knew we were part of a story and she just had to find it out.

Let's hope no one makes trouble for her for telling us what she did."

I started the car and drove to the end of the street and turned left.

"The people who used to come in pairs to see Paula," Flo said, "were they making her pay off what her husband had owed them?"

"It looks that way. And they probably got her started taking equipment from the hospital in order to liquidate the debt faster. But of course after that they owned her. Most likely she's been working for them ever since she got out of Framingham. She may have been running the clinic."

I'd crossed the Fort Point Channel bridge. "Where are we going now?" Flo asked.

"We're going to look for a man in his sixties with no right hand. His name might be Fallon. He could be Paula's father. Maybe he still lives in South Boston. We've got a problem, though."

"You mean all that isn't bad enough already?"

"Finding the man could be easy, if he's still alive."

"So what's the problem?"

"Color," I said. "In Southie black faces are not welcome."

"Even now?" she asked. "Even after busing?"

"Busing may have made things worse in this area."

"Don't you think busing was a good idea?"

"I think if some parents wanted their children taken to a certain public school, then they should have been accomodated, but I know that if anyone had ordered any kid of mine shifted from one school to another when I didn't want it, or my kid didn't, I would have raised Hell."

"But without busing thousands of schools that were once segregated would never have changed."

"Maybe they wouldn't have changed for a long time, but change was already in the air. I like a law that says - You cannot deny a person access because of color. Laws that in just one generation have opened the doors of lunchrooms and universities, of hotels and theaters, of societies and clubs, are good laws. But laws that say - You must admit a given quota of persons because of color - these laws are almost as bad, because they can be counterproductive, as the discrimination they attempt to combat."

"Other black people wouldn't agree with you."

"I know."

"And anything that can put an end to prejudice is to be desired."

"But it's too much to expect it to happen overnight. We've come a long way in a very short time, all the way from slavery to where minorities can attain almost any position in the land. That it still isn't easy is the best part of it. Having things easy is the worst thing that can happen to anyone."

She probably didn't buy that, but she was working on it.

I pulled the car over in front of a police station. It was strictly a No Parking zone. "Take the wheel," I said as I got out. "If you have to, drive around the block. I shouldn't be long."

I went inside. A beefy sergeant at the main desk looked at me over the tops of glasses that had slipped half way down his nose. If he'd put it into words it couldn't have been plainer. The look said - What do you think you're doing here?

I showed him my ID. "I'm looking for a man who's in his sixties. He has no right hand, only a stump. His name could be Fallon. Can you help me?"

The sergeant was still giving me a Get-Lost look. "What's he wanted for?" he asked.

"He's not wanted for anything," I said, "as far as I know. "He may be able to give me some background on a case I'm working on."

"What case is that?"

"I'd rather not say."

"Then I'd rather not help you."

"Look, Sergeant," I said, "there are several good people, all of them white, if that's important, who might be hassled if I start giving out information. Maybe, if I can talk with this Fallon, if that's his name, I can save a number of people a lot of grief."

He was turning it over in his mind. It took time in there, but at last he said, "Try the detective room. In that way," and he pointed where I should go.

Four men were seated at desks when I entered. They were talking, then stopped and stared at me. One got up. "You turning yourself in, Boy?" he asked, approaching me.

"Very funny," I said, and showed him my ID. "The sergeant at the desk said you might be able to help me locate a white male who should be in his sixties and has no right hand."

"Why do you want to find him?"

"I need to talk with him. His name may be Fallon."

"He wanted for something?"

"Not as far as I know. He's probably been living here in South Boston for thirty years. Maybe a lot more. Someone should know him."

"I know him." The man who had spoken was short and bandylegged. He got out of his chair and came across the room. "Follow me," he said and led me through the station and out onto the street. Flo was still parked in front. A cop with curly hair and a mile wide grin was laughing and chatting with her.

"Name's Cantarella," the detective said to me.

"They call me Jeeter," I said. We shook hands.

"That lout at the desk give you a hard time?"

"I'm used to it."

"Yeah. I expect you are."

"Tell me something," I asked. "How did a nice Italian boy like you wind up in the fortress of bigotry?"

He grinned. "Don't you see how dark-skinned I am?" he asked. "Now that they've got me, the station is integrated."

"Or as close as it ever'll get."

"Yeah."

He had started strolling slowly toward the corner.

"It's easier to talk out here," he said. "More private.

"I know Buzzy Fallon. He's a very nice guy. I don't know how you got on to him so fast. You're the one nailed Paula Conway, aren't you?"

He stopped walking and we stood face to face. He was even shorter than I and on those splayed legs his stocky frame looked as unshakable as a three-legged stool.

I nodded. "It's in the papers, I suppose."

"That's right. No names, but reference is made to a 'dusky PI from a nearby metropolitain center.'"

"A few others could fit that description."

"But you show up here only hours after the hearing and you're asking about Paula's uncle. How'd you find him?"

I told him.

"Where do you think this is leading?"

"Can we keep this between the two of us?" I asked.

"If your answer is what I think it will be, a lot of people have probably already reached the same conclusion I have. The media won't get it for a while, but I think the news is already out."

"You may be right. In that case, okay. I think Paula can be tied to Salvatore Pancione. I think Sal wants to go into business on the Cape. He's trying to get his hands on a choice piece of real estate down there. Three parcels. Four owners. Two have been persuaded it's time to sell out. The other two are determined not to sell. I'm working for them. Arson and murder are already part of the picture. Someone is playing for keeps. I think it's Pancione."

"Don't you know that Sal is one of the untouchables? A lot of people won't even speak his name. It's supposed to bring bad luck."

"Sal is bad news and that's his bad luck, not mine. Have you ever met him?"

"I don't even know anyone who has."

"Do you doubt that he exists?"

"I didn't grow up in the North End for nothin'. He's for real. And he's the kind I'd like to see put away. For good."

"Then tell me how to find this Buzzy Fallon who you say is Paula's uncle."

"No one else in the station knows they're related."

"And you don't want them to know. That's why we came outside."

"Right. And the reason for that is, I don't want Buzzy to get hurt."

Cantarella had reasons for reasons that went somewhere way down inside him. I wondered what they could be. He'd opened up as far as he was going to and I could feel him beginning to screw the lid back on again. Probably he had first hand experience with how crime and the law walk hand in

83

hand like brother and sister. They can change places so easily sometimes you can't tell one from the other.

"If I learn anything from Fallon," I said, "and it helps me to get closer to Pancione, Fallon will need protection."

"That's what worries me."

"Could he be moved to another address?"

"He wouldn't move."

"Is there anything you can think of that I could do?"

"Just move fast. If you're on a hot trail, make 'em forget about Buzzy. Then you'll be the one they'll be after."

He gave me the address and told me how to get there. I thanked him and headed for the Buick.

Curly was still giving Flo the benefit of total Irish blarney. He was leaning forward, his arms on the open window and his head almost inside. His butt was up - a real temptation, but all I did was say, "Excuse me, please."

He straightened up. His chin could have rested on the top of my head, kinky hair tickling his Adam's apple. Maybe the same thought had occurred to him. He recoiled, the big Hibernian smile going out like a light when the generator sputters and quits. I got into the car while Flo slipped over to the passenger seat.

"Bye now," Flo said, looking at him sideways through the windshield. She gave him a finger flutter and I drove away.

"Shame on you," I said, "taking advantage of a fine upstanding young fellow like that."

"He was really quite charming," she said. "I haven't heard so much nonsensical malarkey in ages. It was fun. If he was thinking things he shouldn't have, it wasn't my fault."

"That may be stretching the truth a little."

"Well, it was better than driving in circles."

I couldn't deny that. And if female wiles weren't there to be exercised, what were they for?

I drove up the hill, as Cantarella had directed, and turned right and started looking for a place to leave the car. A Lincoln Continental pulled away from the curb ahead of me. It was an old model but in pristine condition. The ruddy face of the driver, a halo of white hair around it, stared at me a moment as I slid into his slot. Maybe it had his name on it. Too bad.

We got out and I locked the car. Two young bucks on the corner were watching us.

I saw which way the street numbers were running, then we set off for Fallon's house.

We found it, a block away. His name was third from the bottom. Had the building been converted into apartments? It was a solid, brick, bow-fronted building and must have been a single dwelling before some speculator got it.

Fallon came downstairs himself, after I rang. Through a sidelight I saw him get out of an elevator and come to open the front door for us. He gave both of us a long careful look.

He had pulled the door wide and stood there with his right hand out of sight. He was quite tall and very thin - a man who had always been slender and who had good bones. His eyes were clear under eyebrows still black, even though the thick hair on his head had gone white.

Cantarella had said, "He won't move," and in the way Fallon faced us I could understand what the detective had meant. This was a man who didn't turn and run. He met whatever came at him, the good and the bad, without flinching or dodging.

"Mr. Fallon?"

"Yes."

"Buzzy Fallon?"

"A few people know me as Buzzy. They're my friends."

"I'm Jeeter," I said. "And this is Mrs. Porter, from Cape Cod. We'd like to talk with you about your niece, Paula."

He drew a breath slowly, giving each of us a nod. Then he said, "Come in."

He led the way. We crowded into the miniscule elevator and he pressed the button for the third floor. When the elevator stopped, he preceded us into his apartment which was spacious and light but crammed with knickknacks and souvenirs and photographs.

"Please make yourselves comfortable," he said. "May I offer you some sherry, or coffee, Mrs. Porter?"

"No thank you," she said.

"Mr. Jeeter?"

"Nothing, thank you."

He sat in an ornate Victorian high-backed rocker. Sunlight came through twin windows to our left and fell on a table covered with bric-a-brack and spilled over onto a rug with curious American Indian designs on it. Dust motes hung in the air and city sounds seemed distant. I could make out blue water over rooftops and chimney pots down the hill.

"Do you bring me news of my niece?" Fallon asked.

"Perhaps you already know that she's been arrested," I said.

He didn't answer right away. His eyes lifted toward something outside the window but I think he was looking inward, not out.

"Yes," he said. "I know she's been arrested. Did you have a part in it?"

"I watched as Paula gave a lethal injection to a man in the hospital who had tried to burn a barn on property adjacent to that owned by Mrs. Porter. She was dressed as a nurse and told the patient, 'Time for your antibiotics.' I've found out that she was once a nurse. Her manner was authentic or I might have caught on in time. My testimony will almost certainly put her away for the rest of her life."

Fallon's deep-set eyes had locked with mine. "And knowing my closeness to her," he said, "you do not hesitate to tell me this?"

"I don't want to hide any painful facts from you," I said. "I hope you will tell us more about Paula, but I don't come to you under false pretenses."

"What do you want me to tell you?"

"You could start with how you are related to Paula."

He took another deep breath. Mrs. Garabedian had put her finger on one of his characteristics. "He always walked real slow," she had said.

I could see he was not to be hurried, yet there was economy of motion in the way he proceeded. He might be slow, but he would move forward on a straight line.

"Paula is my brother's child," he said. "Jack married when he was only nineteen. He was a happy-go-lucky, good-lookin' lad who took anything that came his way, askin' no questions, tellin' plenty of lies. His wife was a pretty young thing, but flighty, and the two of them were in debt up to their armpits before they finished eatin' the cake.

"Jack began stealin' stuff when he was only a boy. With marriage and responsibilities, he turned to armed robbery, got mixed in with some very hard types, had a couple of big years and was caught. The baby was only two years old then, half spoiled already. They sent Jack away for fifteen years. He might have got out in seven, but he was knifed in prison and died. Paula's mother took up with another crook as soon as Jack was sent to jail and she started leavin' Paula with me.

"At first it was only for a day or two at a time, but when she saw I could take care of the child and that the little one was happy with me, she just disappeared. The first years I heard from her once in a while. Then, after 1950, she never wrote again. Maybe she died. The last letter was from Detroit."

"Were you single?" Flo asked.

"I've never married," Fallon said. "Maybe it's just as well."

"So you raised Paula entirely on your own."

"It turned out that way."

He was seated facing us, his left hand holding the stump of the right. He raised it slightly now. "I lost the hand in the Air Force," he said. "I was a pilot on B-24's in southern Italy and sorta wild myself. We used to buzz the villages in the south. That's how I got the name - and a reprimand. Then on the last mission I flew we got shot up pretty bad. I brought the ship in but my right hand was all smashed and had to be amputated. That gave me a one hundred per cent disability pension. I bought this building with three hundred dollars down - mustering out pay. The rents covered expenses and left a bit over. It had been a rooming house until a few years before.

"So I wasn't badly off, and Paula was company. A way to keep busy too. A small child can keep you runnin' all day long for sure. Have you children, Mrs. Porter?"

The question caught her off guard. She blinked. "I have one daughter, Mr. Fallon."

"Then you know how demanding a little one can be. It's a big responsibility. I scarcely noticed the years passing.

"We got along in great style, Paula and I, after she became used to staying here. We played all kinds of games together and I read to her a lot - Mother Goose and Winnie the Pooh at the start and later we got into Saki and JM Singe and even Yeats."

He spoke effortlessly. There was no groping for words. A slight brogue lent color to his speech. His voice was pitched high. I could imagine him singing by the lilt and the rhythm in the way he expressed himself.

"I remember a game we played when she was very small," he said. "I've wondered about it many a time. She'd say, 'Now I'll be your Mother, and you'll be my little boy.' Then she'd care for me and the hand was a fascination for her. She'd pretend I had only just finished getting hurt and she'd bandage the wound and make it well.

"Do you think so little a thing could have been a first step down the long road to becoming a nurse?"

He was looking at Flo who was following every word he spoke. Did she envy this kind gentle man his chance to raise a small girl, the gift of intimacy and interdependence he, not even a father, had been given, while she, a mother, had been denied it?

"I don't know," she answered.

"I've often thought," he went on, "that such small matters might set us in motion in given directions and like a cart rolling downhill it's only the first chance push that determines what will become of us. But then I ask myself - What was it then, that I did, or that I failed to do, so that the cart went careening out of control later and ended crashing and being destroyed?"

He paused again. No doubt he'd asked himself this question many times before. Now he was asking us too. I had no answer for him.

Flo said, "There are too many variables in life, Mr. Fallon. Neither blame nor praise nor responsibility can be laid at any one door."

Would he find any solace in that? It rang of rationalization. I think he saw through it.

"A woman knows things a man can never know," he said, and something passed between them that eluded me. From then on he spoke almost exclusively to Flo.

"Paula did very well in school. She didn't make a lot of friends, though. The friends she did make were often temporary. It could have been because she lived here alone with me and other parents found that unconventional. I think, too, that she felt different, maybe that something was wrong with her because her mother had abandoned her and her father was in prison and then died there.

"She wasn't a pretty girl. She was overweight. A woman would have known how to make her look and feel more attractive. I realized too late I hadn't understood that.

"We remained very close, even as she matured. Her studies took the place of dates and dances and parties that probably should have been a part of her growing up. She made up her mind early that she would become a nurse and she talked and talked about it with me. We scrimped and plotted together through some lean years to put her through her training. It troubled me that neither of us had much of a life outside what we shared, but she seemed to be moving in wider circles when she started work at the hospital."

I was impatient for him to get to what I wanted to know. He was taking his time. Ours too. But in his methodical way he was telling us a lot that was essential to any understanding of what Paula was, and what she became.

"Then one black day she met Pat Conway. She said he came to the hospital in a limousine with another important man to visit a patient of hers. He paid court to her. He invited her out to some swell restaurant. He spent money like he owned the supply. He swept her off her feet. Nothing of the sort had ever happened to her before.

"They had already decided to get married when she brought him here to meet me. I knew in a trice he was no good, but I knew that if I tried to tell her that, she'd hate me. I did my best to get them to hold off so she'd have time to see what he was. It didn't work. They got married before a Justice of the Peace. Never did have a church marriage. Went to live in a two-room flat on East Brookline Street in the South End.

"From one day to the next she was gone. I'll not tell you how empty that left these rooms.

"And it didn't take Paula a week to learn what a mistake she'd made. Pat was a gambler. He played the horses. He'd just won a bundle when he met Paula. I guess he never made a hit that big again. Maybe he was just shrewd enough to know he never would. And there was big steady gullible hard-working Paula. A pushover. A meal ticket. A rock in the river he could cling to whenever the current might have swept him away.

"She knew, but she didn't admit it to me for near a year. She avoided me all that time.

"Then she came here with a shiner one Sunday. He'd belted her. And not for the first time. She told me what a rotter he was and what a fool she'd been. She didn't cry. Perhaps she'd finished crying in a year of loneliness and self-flagellation.

"The sweetness of the small child had gone out of her. The willingness to believe in magic and fairy tale happiness was gone. Her young woman's intensity and dedication to her work had withered. She was old and soured and ugly.

"We never regained the easy laughing ways we had known before. I tried again and again to uncover some of the optimism and lightness that had been part of our times together while she was growing up. It was no good. I could have wept for her, but it was only a memory, a will-o-the-wisp for which I would have cried. The woman she'd become did not inspire compassion.

"Then Pat, they called him Patrick Oh, got beaten. She watched it happen. Right in front of their house. He owed more than three thousand dollars to someone called Ballantine. They made an example of him for any others who might fail to pay up.

"And they still expected to collect. Paula had a job. They put pressure on her. She told me a little at a time when I'd go to visit her. They made her steal equipment from the hospital. Once it was only a question of leaving a certain door unlocked. Another time it meant putting a kind of spectroscope into a laundry cart. I begged her to go to the police, to turn herself in. She wouldn't do it. Did she have larceny in her blood?"

He paused. He didn't seem to be asking either of us.

"I've never felt any temptation to steal," he said, "yet my brother Jack stole from the day he could walk. Paula never stole anything I know of all the time she lived here with me, but after she was made to lift the first machine from the hospital she seemed to take to theft as to the manner born. I noticed things in her flat that I know she hadn't purchased. They say stealing is only a seeking of love. Had she been so deprived of love all those years she and I were together? You're a mother, Mrs. Porter. Would Paula have become a thief if her mother had raised her and given her what only a mother can give?"

"There's no way of knowing," Flo said. "It seems likely that you gave her more than her own mother would have."

"You're a kind woman, Mrs.Porter. I'd like to believe I did all a man could. Still and all..."

He was silent for a while. We didn't push him. A bee flew in through a partially open window. Where had it come from in the city? Were there flowers around the building somewhere? We watched it circle the room and return to the window and tick against the upper portion of glass seeking a way back out. Fallon stood and went to the window and raised it further. With his open hand gently he guided the bee down to the opening so it escaped again. Then he closed the window. It was growing cooler.

"After she got caught and sent to Women's prison in Framingham," he said, standing with his back to us, "I never saw her again. I wrote to her but she didn't answer. I went once to visit. A long trip it was. Either she didn't want to see me or she was afraid for me. I went for nothing. When she was released she didn't come here. I couldn't find where she was. She completely disappeared."

"The mob owned her, Mr. Fallon," I said. "She didn't want you to get involved - the way she'd been roped in."

"Or maybe she'd found her true calling after all."

"Did you ever find out anything about who recruited her or who Patrick's associates were?"

"The only name she ever let slip was that of Ballantine - the one that loaned money to Pat."

"Did you try to locate him?"

"I never did. What could I have done?"

"Do you think Ballantine was someone Pat met at Suffolk Downs?"

"That could be, but I don't know."

I stood up to leave. Flo did too, but she went to Fallon and touched his arm. "Thank you for talking with us," she said.

He turned then and looked down into her wide face. "It's been a pleasure meeting you," he said. "Both of you," glancing my way. "I wish you good luck."

"Take care of yourself," Flo said.

A half smile crossed his face. "Who else?" he asked.

*W*e stepped out onto the street and started back toward the car. A husky teen-ager, almost twenty, had his tail against the car on the passenger side. Another was looking at me, leaning across the top of the car, arms crossed, chin on the back of one hand. Two more were sitting on the steps of the house we'd parked in front of.

"Cross the street," I said to Flo. "Stay out of the way until I signal." She did as I said.

I walked up to the front of the car. "Do you gentlemen mind if I drive away now?" I asked.

The one on the passenger side snickered. "Gentlemen he calls us. I hope he ain't bein' sarcastic. You think he's bein' sarcastic, Jody?"

The one leaning on the car roof said, "Hard to tell with niggers, but it sounded sarcastic to me. Yeah, I think so."

"Don't you know better than to come around here and start insultin' white people, Boy?" It was the first one again. He had both feet on the sidewalk now. He'd pushed off from the car so he was standing free. I stepped around the front of the car and walked to him, arms at my sides.

"I think you've made a mistake," I said. "No one has insulted you."

He'd been ready to back up as I approached, but that would have made him looked bad. I was only six inches from him. He was taller and heavier and many years younger than I. His three buddies must have thought it was not much of a confrontation. Not one had moved. Good.

Casually, he put his left hand against my chest. "Back off," he said, starting to push.

I went a half step backwards drawing him with me. Palm up, I took his left wrist in my left hand and twisted and his elbow came down to where I could grab it with my right hand. Then I rotated it sharply in the same direction so that his body turned away from me as his shoulder got pulled out of its socket. I backed into him then, took his weight over my right shoulder, lifted him off the pavement and flipped him so that he came down on his feet, flying backwards, and went over and his head bounced once on the brick walk and he didn't move again.

By then, the lout on the other side of the car was coming over the top of it at me and the two hunks on the steps were moving too. The one over my head jumped and all I had to do was clip him once in mid-air. He was in a crouch expecting to land on my back. I moved toward him and took a swipe at his feet. He missed me completely and landed on his hands, cracking his skull on the sidewalk, opening a gash in his forehead.

One of the two from the steps tripped over his buddy and pitched forward at my waist. I put my right knee into his face and he did a back cartwheel.

The only remaining warrior pulled up short. Maybe seven seconds had passed. He took a look at the three bodies on the ground, one with a fractured skull, one streaming blood and moaning, the third with a busted neck. He backed up, turned around and jogged out of there.

I wiggled my finger at Flo. We got into the car and drove away.

"Jerry. This is Jeeter again."

I'd stopped at a pay phone back in the South End.

"Yeah. What's new?"

"Everything you've given me so far seems to check out. Pancione and The Senator look like the ones doing the pushing."

"What about this news I been gettin' here? Somethin' about a spade diggin' graves for people all over the Cape?"

"We've got two dead and several casualties, but mostly I just stand and watch. You know how it is."

"Oh sure. Watch, huh? I'd hate to see what'd happen if you got involved."

"Jerry. I've got a name. A money lender. At least he was. Have you ever heard of a guy named Ballantine?"

"Lemme see."

I guessed Jerry was punching one of the PC's in his office. He had a file on everything that could be put under any kind of heading. Probably all he had to do was check 'Sharks' and he'd have an alphabetical list of everyone ever known to have been in that business.

"Here it is, Baby. Ballantine, Giorgio. Active since late 50's. Still around."

"Last known address?"

"Said to be living in Hingham."

"You don't suppose he'd be in the phone book?"

"Not likely."

"But everyone's got a phone."

"So his'll be unlisted."

"Does his name give you any ideas, Dad?"

"Like whaddaya mean?"

"Giorgio is Italian, Ballantine isn't. Suppose his real name is Valentino. Giorgio Valentino."

"Yeah?"

"Do you have a telephone directory there with Hingham in it?"

"Gotcha. I'll see."

I could hear him riffling pages.

"Too many possibilities, Jeeter. There's Valentines and Valentinos, Georges and Giorgios. Anyway, I don't think it's gonna be in the book."

He was probably right. It was interesting, though, that Ballantine lived on the South Shore. So did Pancione.

"Jerry, the nurse was married to a gambler named Conway. Conway was in debt to Ballantine. Somehow I've got to tie these people to Pancione. Do you have any known associates on Ballantine?"

"Hang on a minute," he said.

He was a wizard with computers. I could visualize him tapping orders to the microchip directors of his electronic storehouse.

"Here's something better," he said after a pause. "Here's his whole record."

"Whose record?"

"Ballantine's. Who else?"

"His criminal record?"

"What other kinda record is there? You wanna know maybe when he got his teeth cleaned last?"

"Jerry, how did you get your sticky little paws on a guy's criminal record?"

"I got quite a few of 'em, and how I gottem is nonayer friggen business. You wanna rundown?"

Talk about invasion of privacy! "Just the highlights," I said.

"Yeah. It looks monotonous. Starts at age eighteen. I haven't got his juvenile activities. First arrest was for 'Setting up a Lottery.' Half a dozen of those. Two for 'Assault.' 'Loan sharking,' maybe eight. But here's a biggie. 1973. Together with a Stan Butkowski - 'Murder.' Pleaded guilty to 'Manslaughter' and did two years at Walpole before release on Parole, while Butkowski got fifteen and served nine before release. Looks like he was the one got the short end of the stick. Might be some bad blood there."

"And where does Butkowski come from?"

Another pause, then Jerry said, "He's still on probation and his address is 11 Rutland Square in Boston. You know where that is?"

"I'm only a few blocks away from it right now. Jerry, I don't know what I'd do without you. Someday I'll have to buy you a drink."

"Sure. A pink lemonade."

"Does it have to be pink?"

"Nothin' comes cheap anymore, Son."

"I don't think I could sit in a bar next to a guy sipping a pink lemonade."

"You mean you object to my choice of color?"

"Don't I have a right to draw the line anywhere?"

"Not if yer talkin' with me."

"Jerry, I'll have to give this some thought."

"Do that," he said, and disconnected.

$\mathcal{9}$ got back into the car. Flo looked at me and raised an eyebrow. "Next?"

"Rutland Square," I said. "A man named Stan Butkowski. He and Ballantine were charged with murder in 1973. Ballantine pleaded guilty to 'Manslaughter' and got out in two years. Butkowski did nine. It look as if he was the fall guy. We'll see if there's any pay dirt there when we start digging."

I reached Tremont Street and drove to where we could see the Methodist Church on our left. One block this side of it is Rutland Square, one of the half dozen small parks in the South End where old buildings surround a central area of green, wrought iron railings around trees and shrubbery and flowers.

The only parking place was on the far side of the square, opposite number eleven. You were supposed to have a resident's sticker. Well, we wouldn't be out of the car for long. Or far away from it. I locked up and we walked around to the side where number eleven was. There was even an iron gate into the short walk up to the front door.

I could tell, even before ringing the bell, that the house was empty. It's a sixth sense you develop if you work at it. I rang three times and of course there was no answer. Someone lived there, but no one was at home.

A fellow with a thin beard, wearing old jeans and a green sweatshirt with holes in it was putting leaves and twigs and assorted debris into a plastic bag. He was in front of a house two doors away and he had his eye on us.

"Who are you looking for?" he asked.

"Doesn't Stan Butkowski live here?" I asked.

The fellow set his plastic bag down and walked over to check us out. He was the Neighborhood Watch, I guess. That was all right with me.

"May I ask who you are?"

"You surely may," I said. "This is Mrs. Tercyak, from Polish Profiles. I'm Wilson. Photographer."

"Forgive me for asking, but where's your camera?"

"The Nikkon, and other equipment, is in the car. Some people get nervous if they see me coming, camera cocked."

Maybe he bought it. Maybe he didn't. It didn't matter.

"Better not leave any valuable optical equipment in your car," he said. "We keep our eyes open on the square, but we don't always see everything."

"Thank you. I'll remember that."

"That's okay," he said. "I'm Professor Langley. B. C." He stuck out his hand. "Butkowski's a very private sort of man. He's got a room upstairs here with the family that owns the house, third floor front. He only comes in late at night. Sleeps late in the morning and then goes out again around noon. Sometimes he stays away for several days running."

I looked at Flo. "Then we better come back tomorrow morning," she said.

We thanked the professor and went back to the car and got in.

"Suppose that bearded watchdog had known a few words of Polish?" Flo asked, before I turned the ignition key.

"But he didn't."

"Are you always that lucky?"

"There are good days and there are bad days."

"Is it a good day when you send three young men to the hospital?"

She'd had that question scratching at her ever since we drove out of Southie. How was I to answer? Here was a warm responsive feeling woman who cared about people. She'd been shaken by seeing me hurt those young men, and the others on the Cape.

"I care about people too," I said.

She was looking at me - that way she had of seeing inside and pulling things out of recesses I didn't even know were there.

"I know that," she said. "Partly my distress is the result of sudden exposure to a violent and hateful side of life which I'd never seen before. You aren't the cause of the prejudice that had those boys licking their lips and imagining the fun it would be to beat up a black man. You didn't turn that other Negro into a thug who could be hired by anyone with money to do anything he was told to do. I mustn't blame you for what others are. But maybe..."

"Maybe what?"

"Maybe you could have avoided the violence. Couldn't you have talked your way out of it?"

It was a question that stripped me of all protection.

"You have a tongue just as quick as your hands," she said. "Those boys were only smart-ass adolescents. Couldn't you have got around them with words?"

"I could have tried, Flo. I could have started talking. Often, in tight corners, I've been able to stall, even to walk away from trouble. It's the kind of dilemma cops are faced with every day. How much force is necessary? The thing is - you seldom have a lot of time. A polite debate with established rules would be great, but too often the outcome depends on a split-second decision. If you make the wrong one you seldom get a second chance. If someone has made up his mind to hurt you, words aren't likely to stop him. If someone is already raising his hand to strike you, or is reaching for a weapon, you better get to him first."

"What about running away?"

That was another double-edged question. "I've done that," I admitted. "When you haven't got any chance at all, you try to escape, any way possible. The trouble with running is that you get chased. If you get yourself all tuckered out and then are caught, you're back where you started but you've lost your advantage. Other times you don't have any choice."

"Couldn't you have backed away from those four around the car?"

"Maybe. And maybe you could have returned to Fallon's place and called the police while I was back-pedaling. And maybe they wouldn't have caught me. But they were four young long-legged athletic males. I think they would have overtaken me."

"So you were forced to teach them a lesson. And you enjoyed it."

"Flo, let me ask you a question. You and Huck are paying me because someone wants to take over land you own, presumably in order to turn it into a honkey-tonk playground. Now that we begin to see what kind of people are involved are you ready to turn tail and walk, or run, away?"

"It's not the same thing."

"Isn't it?"

"I don't want to give in to some criminal."

"You choose to stand up for what you believe is right, don't you?"

She didn't answer. I started the car and drove out to Tremont Street and turned right toward Mass Ave. It was getting late in the day. Traffic had thinned out, but a bus went barreling past, Hell bent for Roxbury.

"You know what we forgot to do?" I asked.

"I didn't forget. You were busy."

"Why didn't you say you were hungry?"

"There were more important things than eating."

"Shall we eat now?"

"If you know of a place where we can get a good meal."

I did a U-turn on Tremont and headed back downtown. Five minutes later we were given a table in the Omonia, a Greek restaurant that was a favorite of mine. We had a large salad full of feta cheese and briny ripe black olives. There were *calamari* on the menu, squid, deep-fried. And we shared a bottle of wine labeled Hymettus. It was all new to Flo. She ate with intense pleasure, perspiration beading her upper lip. Even the viscous black coffee met her approval.

When she'd finished everything in sight she leaned back in her chair, her appetite satisfied, and let her eyes meet mine. - What next? they asked.

I'd been trying to work out the answer to that one myself, before it came up. She hadn't said anything about returning to the Cape that evening. We knew that Butkowski wouldn't come in until very late. Mid-morning would be the time to roust him out, if he had come in.

"I could drive you home and come back alone tomorrow," I said.

"Is that what you want to do?"

The fact that I was an employee was becoming uncomfortable. "No," I said.

"What do you want to do?"

103

When a mind reader asks you that kind of question its because she wants to hear you say what she already knows. So you say it.

"I want to spend the night with you."

She was smiling. "For a moment," she said, "I had the feeling you'd rather face five armed bandits than one eager female."

"Did I have a choice?"

"Not this time."

I signaled the waiter and paid and we left the restaurant. The rental car hadn't been tagged even though I'd parked illegally. Maybe this was my lucky day.

I drove to the West End - what used to be the West End. It's all high-rise expensive apartment buildings and condos now. How many thousand southern Italians, Sicilians, Russian Jews, Polish Jews and a dozen other ethnic groups once formed tight neighborhoods here? I could remember the narrow crowded streets, the flat-fronted brick buildings, the variety of tongues you heard spoken as you walked from one section to another. Some very gallant people fought to save the West End, a battle they couldn't win, a cause lost before it started, in the hope of preserving something more American than any condo complex will ever be. They fought for a decade and more and lost, and the city of Boston sent in the bulldozers and the wrecking balls and destroyed forever a small world that had no equal anywhere.

I left the car in a parking garage and we started walking.

"Where are you leading me, Sir?" Flo asked.

"You've put your fate in my hands, fair lady. No questions, please."

She took my arm in both hands and matched her stride to mine. We strolled to the river. The city night was warm and city sounds and city lights were a jumble of whispers and sparkles. We walked out onto the old salt-and-pepper-shaker bridge over the Charles.

I wanted to be sure no one was following us. Also, I love the look of this overgrown town, Boston, across the water, trembling, its reflection upside down in the black river.

"You've come here before," Flo said.

"Many times."

"With other women?"

"Never."

She released my arm and turned to face me. "You still haven't kissed me," she said.

I took her upper arms in my hands. We were almost the same height. Our mouths met. There was the taste of bitter coffee and sugar granules around her lips. I licked it away and a shiver went through her.

We broke apart and turned back toward the city. The Suffolk County Jail, like a great gray owl, hunkered at the end of the bridge and the buildings of the Mass General Hospital rose behind it.

Until we kissed I hadn't decided where I would take her. One of the new anonymous hotels or motels in this part of town would have been safest. It was what she was prepared for, no doubt, but I decided to take a chance.

I walked her along Charles Street and we turned left up Revere. Half way up the Hill I got out my key and we entered one of the taller buildings there. We climbed the stairs to the top and I opened the door to the apartment. I stepped in first and switched on a light.

Flo followed me. She stood beside me, taking in the spare colonial furnishings, the Chinese Imperial rug, the AR speakers with the ten foot rack of LP's, the two modern paintings and the books.

"This is where you live?" she asked.

"I'd like to live here."

"It's not yours?" Disappointed. Confused.

"Oh it's mine, all right. But I seldom come here."

"I don't understand."

"I bought the building several years ago. The other apartments are all rented. I only come here rarely. To hole up. To disappear. Mostly I live in furnished rooms."

"Because of your work."

"Yes. I have to keep moving. There are people who would like to have me dead."

"In the entrance, the name for the top floor was H. Stevens. Is that your real name?"

"No. That's the name of a friend who works in a bank. He manages the building - collects rents, pays bills, sees to repairs. I'd prefer it if you'd forget that name. And the address here."

"This friend won't come barging in, will he?"

"He checks the house once a week, but he has his way of knowing when I'm here."

"Bringing me here could have made you vulnerable."

"Yes."

"You trust me. That's serious."

"It is."

Without warning, tears overflowed her eyes and left shining silver trails on her high cheeks. "No one has shown such faith in me for a very long time," she said.

What made me think of Huck in that moment. Frank Huck trusted her, I was sure. Didn't she know it? Or was it the dead wife that made Huck not trust himself, a loss living on to haunt him, each day and each night a presence felt and

106

missed, a void he wouldn't try to fill even with a woman like Flo? Some people love their sorrows more than life. But Huck wasn't like that. Tom Porter, perhaps, unless he was too thick-skinned even to know when he was hurt. But not Huck.

She opened her purse, found a kleenex and wiped away her tears. "Typical dumb woman who has to cry all the time," she said.

"Not typical," I said. "Not dumb."

"Are tears a sign of weakness?" she asked.

"They can be."

"Do you ever cry?"

"Not in front of my enemies."

"But you do."

"It's happened."

"Was it a sign of weakness?"

"I don't like to think so."

She was walking around the room, peering at books, checking the LP's, touching and lifting things.

"May I look at the rest of the apartment?" she asked.

"Of course."

She went into the corridor. I stepped to the radio and turned it on. Eric Jackson was playing an old record by the Modern Jazz Quartet - Django. He'd gone on to something by Ben Webster by the time Flo finished her tour. She stood in the doorway, hipshot, one shoulder on the woodwork, arms crossed.

"You have a dual personality," she said.

"You mean I'm schizo."

"No. Well...maybe a little."

"Look out. I may be dangerous."

"Oh you are. I know that. But you would also like to be a simple family man - a wife, a house in the suburbs, a couple of kids, some nice dull job with time off for fishing or sailing or hiking."

She was right. Many times I'd dreamed of a life like that. It was a fantasy to soothe me in times of stress.

A thought struck me. An unpleasant thought. Was I just a specimen, a subject of study for Flo?

"You're examining me like something in the lab." I said.

It rang harsh, self-pitying perhaps.

She frowned. Then she dropped her arms and moved close to me. "I'm sorry," she said. "I can't help the way I am. You represent something new to me. I've never even met a black man before. I've never known anyone as quick and effective in any kind of contest as you are. This fascinates me and yes, I'm collecting data. It's the kind of thing I've been doing for years and years. But it's the human being you are who draws me nearer every minute. I'm more than a little frightened and I'm gabbling like some silly hen because I'm not thinking of consequences, or don't want to, because I guess I've lost my head over you."

A long time later I came awake with my left arm tingling. Flo's head was on that shoulder. Her left leg and half her body rested on me in my narrow bed. I moved the arm out from under and got some circulation going again.

In the other room the radio was still playing. Night Air - WGBH. A harpsichord playing. Bach. The English Suites, I guessed. My clock read 3:49.

When a shrink goes to bed with a client, shouldn't he be sent up for ten-to-twenty? What about a private eye? Wasn't there some ethical stardard I violated here. I didn't want to look at it too closely.

Flo's breathing changed. She was awake.

"Did something disturb you?" she asked.

"My arm was asleep. I had to move it."

Enough light came through the window so that I could see her face. It was a face I'd carry with me far into the future, eyes set wide apart, eyes that mostly stayed open and missed very little. She practised no artifice - no plucking of eyebrows, no eye-shade, no make-up. Her skin was smooth and clear. She had small ears and a strong nose, even teeth, mouth and lips full and questing.

I pushed the covers back so I could see her again, her body pale and luminous against mine, left breast warm and soft on my chest.

"I like it when you look at me," she said. "Your eyes walk on me like fingers dancing. I can almost feel it where you look."

Her short auburn hair on the pillow was an ink-black shadow and the dense dark shadow under the rising mound of her belly was a black bush on a moonlit field.

I let my hand follow the line, dipping and rising again, from hip to waist to rib-cage to nipple-tipped breast. I wanted to lose myself in this woman forever. I thought that sex and love, for a time, could be one. Maybe escape from the ineluc-table aloneness every human suffers could be found in the meeting of two bodies if one could at last give all of oneself. At least for an hour. For half and hour?

Before daybreak, we made love again. We came close to passing through those invisible vitreous barriers that keep us separate from each other. Locked together, coupled and spent, in sleep maybe we reached a few moments of oneness. That's as near as you ever come. Then a new day dawns and you're two again.

9

It was ten-thirty when I double-parked on Tremont Street. We walked a block and a half to get to Rutland Square. I preferred not to be seen by that Boston College professor again, if possible.

No one answered the bell until I rang for the third time. The door opened on a knobby-jointed, long, somnambulist in a T-shirt, with pants hastily pulled on, slippers on his feet.

"Mr. and Mrs. Gillespie won't be back until the middle of the week," he said.

"We're not looking for them," I said.

"Who are you looking for?"

"You," I said. "Stan Butkowski."

"And what do you want with Stan Butkowski?"

"Talk. Some friendly conversation."

"You're a cop."

"Just a private investigator." I showed him my ID.

"Come back some other time," he said, and started to close the door.

I said, "No. We're coming in now, Stan." I put my hand on the door. He moved his right foot back and planted it.

"Don't even think of it, Stan," I said. "Sal might not like it."

He froze. The name meant more to him than I could have hoped. We entered the hallway and I closed the door behind us.

"Since no one else is in the house," I said, "why don't you lead the way to your room and we'll have a quiet talk. Okay?"

He was off balance. He was awake now but he didn't know who we were or what we wanted. He'd been in prison for nine years. That conditions a man to do what he's told and to ask no questions. He led us upstairs to a big room at the front on the third floor.

Linoleum. A bed in disarray against one wall. Refrigerator and two-burner gas plate against the other. One straight-backed chair by a cheap table. Racing forms on the table. A make-shift closet in the corner. A dresser and a mirror. Not much better than a cell. A little bigger. And he could come and go.

Flo sat on the chair by the table. Stan sat on the bed when I told him to. I stood by the bay window where I could see the Square.

"A man named Fallon," I said, watching Stan. "Patrick Oh. He owed money to Ballantine. Couldn't pay. Took a beating. What do you know about that?"

"Nothing."

"Stan," I said. "Let's keep it friendly. It's a nice day. The sun is shining. In a little while you'll have breakfast maybe, if you still have a face to feed. Don't lie to me. Understand?"

There was hatred in his look. Fear too. He was one of those poor dumb types who'd been pushed around all his life. Some quirk of destiny, no doubt, had determined he'd go into crime instead of bricklaying, or clerking, or manual labor. He'd never been anybody and never would be. But he'd survived. Cunning and quick, like a rat in a cellar, he'd spent his life escaping. Just barely.

"So how about it, Stan?" I said.

"What do you want to know?"

"You and Ballantine worked together. It'd be more than ten years ago now. Did you help beat up Fallon?"

"There's a statute of limitations on that, isn't there?"

Answer a question with a question. He was slippery. Maybe not as dumb as I thought.

"Nobody's thinking of bringing charges now," I said. "Did you, or didn't you?"

"How do I know you or the dame here isn't taping this?"

"No tapes. In fact, if you give me what I want, you'll never see me, or the *lady*, ever again. Or hear from us either. But I am going to get what I want out of you. You can make it pleasant, or you can make it painful. That's the only choice you've got."

He glared at me. He was sweating. The smell of stale bedding and unwashed armpits and dirty socks filled the room.

"They'll kill me if I talk to you," he said.

"Not if they don't find out you talked."

"They'll know. They always know."

"Maybe they'll be too busy by then to waste any time on you."

He thought about that. He liked the idea. "Who are you working for?" he asked.

"That's my affair," I said. "And you're my affair. Now are you gonna open up or should I get out a blade and open you up?"

He shuddered. For once, the myth of 'every nigger's got a straight razor on him' was going to serve a purpose.

"So all right," he said. "I was one of the guys beat up Fallon. Fallon was a dead beat. A welcher. He had it coming."

112

"Who was with you?"

"I forget."

Getting anything out of this guy was like walking in wet clay with hip boots on.

I took a step closer to him. "Stan," I began...

He put his arm in front of his face as if I had been on the point of striking him. "Okay," he said. "It was Marrs. Benny Marrs."

"And where is Marrs now?"

"He moved to Fitchburg. That's all I know. They said he moved to Fitchburg."

He was telling the truth at last.

"Was that when Ballantine started working with you?"

"Right after that. Yeah."

"You were an enforcer and you worked in pairs. Right?"

"There was always two of us. Some guy didn't pay up, we'd knock out a few of his teeth, break an arm, leave a few scars."

"But Ballantine was a money lender. How come he switched?"

"He got switched. He got stuck too many times. They told him to do his own dirty work if he couldn't pick a moocher we could squeeze and get results.

"And he didn't like that."

Stan didn't like admitting it either. His job was bottom of the ladder. Muscle. Mop up.

"So in 1973 the two of you beat up a guy and he died. Right?"

"I never killed anybody," Stan said. "Ballantine killed him. He wore a steel tip on his work shoes. He kicked the guy in the head when he was already unconscious. His head was against the curb. Ballantine kicked him just in front of the left ear. One of the guy's eyes popped clean out of the socket. I saw the boot go in up to the lacings. The skull was caved in like a Halloween pumpkin."

Flo had paled.

"But you got sent up for fifteen," I said, "and served nine, and Ballantine only did two. How come?"

He looked at me as if I'd lost my marbles. He didn't bother to answer. I guessed Ballantine had been more important to the organization than Stan. Some money changed hands, plea bargaining, orders to Stan to keep mum. Shafted again.

"Where's Ballantine living now?" I asked.

"You aren't ever gonna say you saw me?"

"Not if you tell me the truth."

"And why should I believe you?"

"Because there's a code some of us live by."

"And you're one does that?" Did he wish he could understand something this strange? The only code he'd ever lived by said, Look out for number one.

"Ballantine lives in Carver."

"I thought he lived in Hingham."

"That was a long time ago."

"Address?"

"That I don't know."

"Then how do I find him?"

"He goes under the name of George Vale."

"So his real name is Valentino? Italian?"

"Could be. I'm no expert on nationalities."

"And he's still working for Sal."

"You're the one that says so."

"Is he or isn't he?"

"As far as I know."

"In what capacity?"

"Huh?"

"Is he enforcing again, or is he loan sharking?"

"He's loan sharking. Another assault charge could put him away forever."

"And he gets his orders from Salvatore Pancione."

"Just like always."

"Where does Sal live?"

Stan lifted his head to look at me, the black stubble on his bony jaw catching points of sunlight as it came through the window.

"He's the one you're really after, isn't he?"

I didn't answer.

"You're gonna get killed," Stan said.

"Just tell me where Sal lives," I ordered.

He kept me waiting. I could almost hear the thoughts dropping into place inside his head.

"He lives in Scituate. Like a king."

"Address?"

"I don't know. Ballantine knows. He was there once."

"You still see Ballantine?"

"Never. I'm not supposed to associate with known criminals. You know that."

"What do you do with your time?"

"Is that any business of yours?"

"In case anything you've told me isn't one hundred per cent accurate, I'll be back to see you, Stan. You're out at Suffolk Downs most days, right?"

He slumped again.

"Right."

"And where are you working?"

"I'm at the Statler. Nights. Eight to four. I do halls."

Was there anything else I could get out of him? It didn't seem likely. I let Flo walk most of the way downstairs before I followed her. Stan was still sitting on the edge of his rumpled bed when I closed the door to his room.

On Park Square I exchanged the Buick for a Pontiac. The adolescent clerk asked if there was anything wrong with the Buick. I told him No everything was fine. "I just like trying them all, as long as the company's paying. Someday I might buy one."

"Nothin' like havin' your own wheels," the kid said.

He probably had some battered relic he'd been working on for years. There was oil and grime in the creases of his palms that no amount of soap could wash away.

"What do you drive?" I asked.

"Got me a '61 T-bird, Man. Dual carbs. Quadraphonic sound. Make out like a bandit, if ya know what I mean."

"Guess I do," I said, and gave him a wink. "Just stay clear of the jail bait."

"Nothin' but older women for me, Man. They like a young one and I like 'em experienced and horny. Can't beat it."

"Beats beating it, too."

"You better believe it."

Flo had gone to phone Tom while I was switching cars. She came to the desk then and found the kid grinning like a fool. The grin faded and turned into a leer as Flo approached. When she put both hands on my upper arm his mouth dropped open.

"Bandits come in all sizes, Son," I said. "And all colors."

I took the keys out of his hand and we left. You could tell that none of those 'older women' he'd been escorting had been in a class with Flo.

*W*hen I got onto the Expressway going south I asked Flo how Tom had reacted.

"He was resigned," she said. "I told him I was with you and that you were making progress. He didn't seem to care. He didn't ask any questions. He said everything was quiet at home. I told him we'd probably get back by tonight, otherwise I'd call again. 'Be careful,' he said, and hung up."

She sat close beside me, looking down the road ahead.

"Tom is vain and selfish," she said, "but he's hurting just the same. What a vulnerable species we are!"

"Isn't that also one of our qualities?"

"But it's a failing too. Compassion will be the undoing of the human race."

I'd thought that myself, sometimes.

"Without it, though," I said, "we'd all be Stan Butkowskis. We could beat up on anybody anytime and feel nothing."

We were traveling at a steady sixty-five. Traffic was light. It was one of those September days when the sun is lower in the sky but the warmth of summer just past still lingers and the light has that extra clarity a chill night bequeathes.

"Are you having regrets?" I asked.

"No," she said immediately. "No. Tom's had it coming. It could even do him good to begin to know what it means to be left out."

She didn't add anything. I thought I knew what she meant. When she was ready, she'd talk about her child. I'd wait.

I made the turn off for Carver. It was only one o'clock when we reached that town. We had a sandwich and coffee at a roadside stand. I checked the local phone book and found an address for George Vale. The blowsy dame behind the counter told me how to get there.

"This could begin to get tricky," I told Flo. "You've got Tom's revolver in your purse. If there's trouble, don't be reluctant to use it."

The house was a split-level ranch on a half acre lot, a carport to the left, shake siding, neat lawn and standard landscaping. The snazzy Corvette in the drive was out of place since the neighborhood was decidedly lower middle class. Corvettes are for sports - and rich blokes.

I pushed the button. Chimes dinged inside. A woman opened the door. She was somewhere between fifty and sixty. She could have been a guard at Framingham - gray hair, gray face, gray shapeless dress on a body like the trunk of a tree.

"Yes?" she said

"Mrs. George Vale?" I asked.

"Yes."

"We're from the Carver Civic Association. Your husband has been nominated for Treasurer of our group. Could we speak with him?"

She gave me the kind of look a banker gives you when you ask for a one hundred fifty thousand dollar mortgage on a one hundred and twenty thousand dollar house.

"I don't think he'd be interested," she said.

"We rather expected that, Mrs. Vale, but the committee felt that Mr. Vale's special qualifications..."

"He wouldn't want it, I'm sure." She began to close the door.

"Who is it, Peg?" The voice was a rasping baritone.

"Some committee that **says** they want you for..."

"Lemme take care of it."

Mrs. Vale stepped aside as a hirsute ape of a man padded across the rug to the door. He was naked except for the pelt that covered him from neck to ankle and down to his wrists. He'd been in the shower and was still dripping. He left big bear-like tracks on the wall-to-wall carpeting.

"Whaddaya want?" he asked.

The average man is self-conscious about being naked before strangers. This one was as at home in his shaggy skin as any cat or dog is in its own back yard.

"Giorgio Valentino," I said. "That's what we want."

His eyes narrowed. "You're the one from the Cape," he said. "You're the one grabbed Paula, ain'tcha?" He had barely glanced at Flo. "Whyn'tcha step right into the parlor. This is too good to be true."

He opened the door all the way and stood to one side so we could enter. Flo started to draw back. I took her arm and guided her inside. The door clicked shut behind us.

"So you're lookin' for Giorgio Valentino," he said. "Well, here he is. In all his glory." He lifted his arms away from his sides, standing legs apart, genitals swinging free under a heavy paunch, hairy breasts quivering.

He was fat and repugnant, but he'd be hard to hurt. There was still a lot of muscle under all the lard.

"Siddown," he said. "Make yourselves comfortable."

"We're not going to sit down, George," I said. "You're allowed to, if you wish."

His mouth opened into what he must have thought was a comic's O. "What's this?" he said. "Some skinny, flea-bitten Jig is gonna tell me what to do in my own house? You a funnyman?"

"Sometimes they laugh," I said. "Sometimes they cry. Usually in that order."

"Hey. I like it. Ho, ho, ho. Now whyn't ya try for part two. Okay?"

"I hate to keep you waiting," I said, "but first tell me how you know about Paula."

"I should save you for dessert, eh? Like you was some kinda chocolate eclair."

He laughed at what he though was a very sharp quip.

I just stared at him.

"You don't think I'm amusing? You're supposed to laugh at my jokes. You tryin' to annoy me?"

"You're hilarious, Giorgie. Now tell me about Paula.

The 'Giorgie' was too much for him.

"Peg," he said. "Go call for transportation for this crud. Straight to the hospital he's goin'."

Mrs. Vale was in the open doorway to the kitchen. She turned and disappeared. Flo caught my eye. I dropped my eyes to her purse. She understood and followed Mrs. Vale.

The big guy hesitated. He'd missed something, but he didn't know what and he wanted me.

120

He charged. I feinted left and dodged right and he never touched me. He pulled up like a bull that's gone through the cape and hit nothing but air while the man has disappeared. Bewildered, snorting, he turned slowly to look back. In the silence, he realized he wasn't hearing any phone conversation.

He pivoted to go check on his wife.

Like many fat men he had short spindly legs. For a second I was behind him and his weight was on his right leg as he started to step toward the kitchen.

I swung a roundhouse kick at him parallel to the floor and caught the outside of his right knee. The leg snapped and he went down. He turned to get up and screamed as the knee folded sideways and torn ligaments ripped loose.

I stepped around him and looked into the kitchen. Mrs. Vale was seated on the floor, back against the refrigerator, and Flo was opposite her, perched on a kitchen chair, both arms on a formica table, her two hands holding Tom's loaded and cocked revolver.

"Nice going," I said. "Keep her right there."

I turned back to Vale - Ballantine - Valentino. He was trying to crawl to the fireplace where there were tongs and a cast iron poker.

"Hold it right there," I said. "You move again and I'll fix the other knee too."

He rolled onto his left side. He was in agony and looking at his lower leg which lay at right angles to his thigh didn't improve his mental state.

"You crippled me," he sobbed.

"Just the way you crippled a lot of other helpless slobs."

"I'll never walk again."

"You're breaking my heart."

He snarled like a pit bull. "You better kill me," he said. "If you don't, I'll hunt you down. I'll get you. Someday. Somehow. You fucking dirty black bastard."

"I'll hear you coming, Georgie. Ga-thump, ga-thump on your gimpy pins. Forget it. You're through."

If he'd been able to get his hands on me, he would have torn me apart, tooth and nail. Only his hatred was keeping him from collapse.

"I want to know about Paula," I said, "and you are going to tell me."

"I'll tell you shit."

"Not likely," I said. "I wouldn't allow that."

I stepped around him and picked up the poker, just in case. It was a cheap one, but it was a substantial piece of iron.

"Paula was married to Patrick Oh," I said. "Pat borrowed money from you. He got in over his depth. Butkowski and Marrs beat him unconscious. Then the organization moved in on Paula. They forced her to make good on the three thousand Pat owed you. Once she started working for them she couldn't back out and maybe she began to feel at home. They let her set up the clinic. She was boss and loved it. Isn't that right?"

"So if you know it all, why are you buggin' me?"

I'd pulled that last one out of thin air and tried it for size and his reaction made me feel certain I'd guessed close to the truth.

"Where's the clinic, George? That's one thing I want to know."

"If I knew, I wouldn't tell you. And I don't know."

His color was bad. I was afraid the pain was going to make him pass out.

"You might get lucky and get taken there. Or is it too far away to do you any good?"

"Go fuck yourself."

"Shall I phone for transportation. Peg was going to place a call. It could have been for some goons to come after me. Maybe in a fake ambulance. Where's the phone book Georgie?"

He didn't answer. There was a phone book somewhere - not the one the company issues. It might take a little time to find it.

Keeping an eye on George, I stepped back to the door to the kitchen. I asked Flo to hand me the gun. When I had it I told Mrs. Vale to get on hands and knees, no feet, and crawl into the room with her husband.

A wall phone was next to the stove.

"Find a kitchen knife, Flo," I said, "and cut the cord off the phone. I need a four-foot length to tie up this gray lady."

Flo rummaged in a couple of drawers and found a knife. Quickly, she cut and brought me a piece of phone cord. I fixed Mrs. Vale so she wouldn't be able to go anywhere without help.

There wasn't enough cord to tie up George too. I handed Flo the revolver again and took the knife and cut the dual lead to the TV. That antenna wire is about as tough as anything needs to be. I made George roll onto his gut. I put my knee in the small of his back and lashed his hands together. He lost consciousness before I was through.

"Keep the gun on them, Flo," I said.

I went into the master bedroom and was about to start going through bureau drawers when I noticed George's clothes flung onto the bed. An inside jacket pocket held a booklet that was going to be worth plenty. It listed names and addresses. By each name was an amount in dollars. Then followed a series of dates, one week apart. A check mark clearly meant that payment had been made. A zero was self-explanatory. An X could have meant a beating. Sometimes after an X, payment resumed. PIF stood for Paid In Full - end of transaction.

Six phone numbers on the last page looked special. Were they those of enforcers, or were they for others in the organization, higher-ups?

I had the feeling George really didn't know where the clinic was or how to contact it. But one number was circled in heavy red ink. Emergency? The boss? I'd have to work fast to track all this stuff down before the word went out that I had it.

There was one other thing I needed. It would be in a secure place and it would be fireproof. The bedroom wouldn't hide it. I gave a hurried look into the bath and kitchen and study. Not likely. The carport wouldn't do either. Stairs led to the cellar from the kitchen. I went down into a damp musty-smelling cinderblock cave. The heating system was there - forced hot air. There was an electric hot water heater. Closets. The usual accumulation of little-used or discarded items - cartons, yard tools.

Against the rear wall, behind piles of magazines, someone had built a cinderblock enclosure. It had a steel door and was locked. I went back upstairs and got the keys I'd seen in George's pants pocket. One of them opened the steel door. Inside was a metal box and several books of records. I took it all up to the kitchen. One of the keys opened the metal box. It was full of money. I didn't bother counting it, but there was a lot, ten thousand dollars at least.

Probably none of these things could be used as evidence in court, but evidence they were and the authorities would be glad to have them. One thing about stealing from criminals - they don't call the cops. I put everything into a shopping bag. Flo put her gun back in her purse. We left the happy couple side by side on the wall-to-wall and took off.

*B*ack in Boston, I turned in the Pontiac and picked up my own car again. I figured it would be at least a couple of hours before the Vales could get loose. So far, no one had picked up our trail. They'd be looking for a Pontiac or a Buick, if they were looking at all.

We made it back to the Cape in just over one hour and I drove straight to the station. Luckily, the Chief was in.

"Frank Huck came by an hour ago," he said, looking from Flo to me to Flo again. "Tom told him you phoned from Boston. Frank wondered if it was on the level. You all right, Mrs. Porter?"

"I'm fine," she said.

The Chief had other questions but he didn't ask them.

I emptied the shopping bag onto his desk - the money box, the booklets of loan records, the keys. I hadn't thought of it before, but the keys to the Corvette were on the key ring too. Did our boy have a duplicate set? I hoped not.

"An anonymous donor left these with you," I said. "Looks like a loan shark operation. The money hasn't been counted. Having been obtained, presumably, without a warrant, these items are probably useless as evidence in court. On the other hand, they could be very useful in any plea bargaining, or in dickering with certain malefactors."

"Did the 'anonymous donor' remove this material from some person's home?" the Chief asked.

"To the best of one's knowledge, the material came from the home of Mr. and Mrs. George Vale of Carver, Massachusetts," I said. "George Vale is a name used by a man known as

Ballantine, aka Valentino, and probably originally named Giorgio Valentino, who served two years of a longer sentence for murder and who is assumed to be associated with Salvatore Pancione."

The Chief's mouth had taken on a puckered look. "Did the aforementioned Mr. Vale offer any resistance when his home was, shall we say, invaded?"

"There appears to be some confusion as to what transpired within the Vale home. Apparently, Mr. Vale tripped on the livingroom rug and twisted his knee."

Flo was shaking her head as much as to say, I don't believe this.

"Chief," I said, "There are some phone numbers here." I turned to the phone numbers I'd found in the booklet in George's jacket. "If you can tie each of these to an address, starting with the one circled in red, we may find ourselves right inside the operation that's after property here in town. I wouldn't want anyone alerted by phoning direct, but certainly you can get authorization to connect each number to a name and a place even if the numbers are unlisted. Right?"

"There's always a way, if there's enough reason."

"Would breaking up a stronghold of organized crime be reason enough?"

"Federal authorities could be called in on that."

"We've got a murdered man and the murderess already, both from inside the organization."

"I'll get you the names and addresses," the Chief said. "It shouldn't take more than an hour. Will you be back at the Porter's?"

"We'll go there now," I said.

"Mrs. Porter," the Chief said as we got up to leave.

Flo turned back to him.

"Mrs. Porter, there's a sizeable heavy metal object in your purse. I would not like to find out that you are carrying a weapon without a permit."

We headed back to the car in a hurry.

om wasn't at the house. No sign of Seelye either. An unfamiliar car was in Huck's drive. I left Flo and walked over to find out who it was.

Voices. In the barn. I looked in. The horse lay on its side. Huck and another man were beside it. When I blocked the light, standing in the door, they looked up and stopped talking.

I walked in. "Dead?" I asked.

There was no need for an answer. When I was close enough I could see that the animal would never move again.

Huck introduced me to the second man, a veterinarian named Benny Sikorha.

"I came back from the shop thirty minutes ago," Huck said. "He was still breathing then. By the time Benny got here, it was all over."

"What did it?" I asked.

"Massive injection of any of a number of drugs. I'll have the answer by tomorrow. The needle went in here." Benny indicated a spot near to where the saddle usually lay.

"You mean someone just walked, or drove, in here, gave the horse a shot over the partition, and then left?"

"It looks that way," Huck said. "No one was around." His voice lacked the resonance it should have had. This was another needless death, for him. He was shaken. Where there should have been anger there was only pain. The third member of the quartet was ready to cave in. If Flo were to capitulate, the property would be up for grabs.

I stepped back out into the sunlight. An immense quiet lay on the land. The sun's rays, almost horizontal, were burnt sienna and ochre laving the still grasses of the marsh. A harrier dipped and turned above phragmites. The barn's shadow stretched almost to the Porter's dock. Wood smoke. Ground fog forming. Night's chill crouched, ready to spring.

A vehicle came up the Porter's driveway. A UPS truck. It beeped as it drew up by the side door. Flo Porter came out.

I was running and yelling but it was two hundred yards over hummocks and ditches and a stone wall.

Too late, Flo heard me. They grabbed her. There were at least two of them. The truck went up on the lawn, wheels spinning, tore apart a bed of flox and coleus, headed out the drive and was already turning onto the state road by the time I got to my car.

Had Huck heard me? Would he have the sense to phone the police without waiting even a second? Did he get a look at the truck?

I lost precious seconds starting the car, turning, getting to the end of the driveway. The truck had gone out of sight headed west.

I gunned the motor and then started thinking. Slow it. A UPS truck exceeding the speed limit would be noticed quickly. And remembered. There had to be a second vehicle standing by. They'd switch. They could already have ducked into a side street.

On the next curve, I passed a road leading into a development. The tail of the truck was just disappearing down it. I braked. A car behind me went into the embankment to avoid crashing. I U-turned. The guy rolled down his window and yelled choice epithets at me. He had good reason to.

The fresh black top of the development road was as smooth as the top of a table. Lot numbers were posted along each side. Forty-seven more houses would be built here in a matter of months. Forty-seven more septic systems. About a hundred more cars and vans. Two hundred more people. Dogs. Cats. Bicycles and motorbikes. Demand for more schools, more cops, more hospital space, more services of all sorts.

There was a turn around at the end of the road. The truck was there. Two men were heaving Flo's inert body into the back of an '85 Olds. One got in back with her and slammed the door. The second ran to the other side and got in next to the driver as the car started up and headed straight at me. I spun the wheel and hit the brakes and came to a stop broadside across the road.

The other car didn't stop. It was probably only going twenty miles an hour when it hit my front end, but I was half out of it on the far side when the whole car rose up and banged into me, knocking me flat. Before I could recover, two guys were on top of me. I felt a needle go through my shirt into my arm. For a long time after that I didn't remember anything.

*T*otal darkness. Pain. It felt like a broken rib, upper left side. I moved to touch the spot, but my hands were immobilized. Feet too. I remembered having my right foot still in the car, left foot on the ground, then the car swinging at me as its front end got smashed by the Olds. The half open door must have caught me in the side. I could breathe all right. Maybe it was more laceration than broken bones.

I lay still. I sensed another person near me - the faint thin sibilence of controlled breathing.

"Flo?"

"So it is you. I could feel that someone else was in here, but I didn't know who. Not for sure."

"Have you been conscious long?"

"It seems like a long time, but maybe it's only been minutes."

"Are you hurt?"

"No."

"In any way?"

"No one's touched me, except to give me a shot."

"Nembutol."

"That's what I thought too. I was afraid they'd given you too much."

There was enough concern in her voice to make my eyes water. It had been a long time since anyone had much cared if I lived or died.

"Any idea where we are?" I asked.

"Not the slightest."

"The sun was just setting when they gave me my shot." I told her about chasing the truck and how they smashed into my car. "If it's near midnight we could be up to one hundred and fifty miles from your home. Or we could be quite close. Did you get a look at the men in the truck?"

"Only one. When the truck drove up to the house and sounded its horn I went out thinking it was a routine delivery of something I'd ordered. The man who came toward me had a package and a clipboard in his hands, but he wasn't the driver I expected. He was over thirty, needed a shave. I'd remember him if I saw him again. I was stupid not to realize what was happening. When I heard you yell it was too late."

"Don't blame yourself, Flo. A lifetime of trusting people is no preparation for dealing with criminals."

The high distant drone of a jet reached us. It could have been a 747 in, or out, of Logan, or maybe a military plane from Otis. And somewhere I was sure I could hear a semi whining down a highway. Otherwise, we were surrounded by silence, a silence that was oddly dense. We were indoors. I could feel walls around us. Was it a cellar? There was cement under my face, but no matter how I strained my eyes I could make out no light. Any window, even a crack by a door, would have let in some dim glimmer. All cellars had a window or two. A closet? This place felt large for a closet. How about a storage shed? That might fit.

"Can you move at all?" I asked.

"I can roll over. My hands and feet are taped."

"It feels like industrial tape. Very rugged stuff."

"Should I try to get closer to you?"

We were speaking just above a whisper, but if there was a microphone in the room, or shed, someone would have heard us already. No one had come. That anyone might be close seemed unlikely. They'd chucked us into a place from which escape would be impossible, bound as we were, and they'd gone off to sleep in a comfortable bed somewhere else.

"Come over here if you can. I can't roll very well. I may have a cracked rib."

There was the sound of knees and elbows bumping the concrete and then her head was against my thigh.

"Use my leg for a pillow," I said. "You must be pretty stiff by now. This floor could be softer."

"What about you? And you're injured, too?"

131

"We can take turns. This'll get the kinks out of your neck."

Our hands were taped behind us making it impossible to lie on our backs for more than a few minutes at a time. The only alternative was to lie on our sides, but that put the neck at a painful angle. My hands were swollen and hurting from lack of circulation. At least there was still feeling in them.

"I need to go to the bathroom," Flo said.

"There goes my pillow," I said.

She snickered. "Don't make me laugh. It'll be all the sooner."

I needed to go, too. Physical discomfort was going to become acute as the hours passed. I wondered if we were within hearing of other dwellings or a roadway. Would shouting for help do any good? It was odd that we weren't gagged if cries for help could serve any purpose. Probably we were somewhere out in the country. Isolated. Still, I was on the point of saying we should try it when I heard a car approaching. It shifted gears as if coming up a steep incline. Stopped. Garage doors were opened close to us. The car entered the garage and the motor was cut. We were in a chamber attached to the garage.

"Turn on the lights," a male voice said.

Blinding light struck us. We were surrounded by poured concrete. No window. A steel door only arm's length from my head. An overhead bulb lit every corner of our cell. Ten-by-eighteen, maybe. The size of two cells.

Someone put a key in a padlock, undid it and pulled it out of what was probably a double hasp. A key went into the lock in the door. The door swung open barely missing my head.

The first man to enter was the one who had slung Flo's unconscious body into the back of the getaway car. Behind him was a man I couldn't be sure of, but I guessed he had been the driver. There was no one else.

"Would you look at that," the first one said. "All cuddled up like babes in the wood."

"Looks more like she's ready to give him a blow job."

This one was small, with squinty eyes and big ears.

"That's what is wrong with you, Gill. You have no sense of poetry."

"Poetry, shit. How about we show this broad what poetry is." He started to open his fly.

"Gill, you are not going to last in this organization if you cannot control your baser instincts."

Gill shut his mouth then, but what went on in his Neanderthal brain knew no restraint, that was plain to see.

"So," said the one in charge. "What we have here is two customers to be delivered to the man who says Do and Don't. How are you feeling, Dear Lady?"

"I desperately need to go to the bathroom," Flo said.

"Rest stops were not included in our instructions," the man said. "However, the boss wouldn't want the limo soiled." He produced a pocket knife and snapped open the blade. He leaned over and cut the tape binding Flo's feet. Slowly, she got to her knees and then stood unsteadily.

"The hands, too," she said. "Please."

"I'll show you the way first," he said, and stepped through the door. "The toilet's in there," I heard him say. "You can close the door. Don't lock it."

"The hands?" Flo said again.

"There you are," he said. "Better not remove all the tape. It'll hurt. And we'll be taping your wrists again in just a minute."

When they came back, the big guy looked at me. "You too, I suppose."

"I can't hold out much longer."

He grabbed my arm and lifted me onto my feet. The pain where I was injured almost made me pass out. That, and suddenly being upright.

"Hey, you're hurt." He unbuttoned my shirt and looked. Gently he touched the spot where the car door had sliced into me. "May need an X-ray to be sure," he said. "Some torn pectoral muscles. Bone bruises. I don't think anything's broken."

"Are you an MD?" I asked.

"I'm working at it."

Was he part of the clinic? I wanted to ask more, but he probably wouldn't have answered. He cut the tape on my wrists and helped me to hop to the can. He didn't let me out of his sight.

The garage was oversized. Or maybe it only seemd so because it contained none of that clutter of equipment and oddments that always accumulates in garages.

The car that had crashed into mine was there. Its front left fender had been damaged some and hastily beaten back into shape. The left headlight was new. It was an '82 Olds. Black. My little Toyota had been no match for it. I wondered where it was now and if I'd ever get it back.

We returned toward the cell where Flo and I had spent the last four to six hours. I looked in. Gill was crouched in front of Flo, who had her back to the wall.

"If you even touch me," she hissed, "I'll claw your eyes out."

She was like a cat, back arched, hackles raised, nails unsheathed. The little guy with the big ears was about to be ripped to pieces.

Instead, the other man stepped around me and backhanded Gill, knocked him up against the cement wall where his head bounced once. He sank to his knees, blood oozing from his forehead. "You're gonna drive us back to the compound," the big man said, "and after that you're through. You got that? Now get up and get into the car."

Who was this person? He could be courteous, gentle, considerate. I couldn't figure him out. Why was he part of this organization?

He pulled a roll of tape out of his jacket and asked Flo to put her hands behind her.

"Could you tape them in front of me?" she asked. "I'm still hurting from having my shoulders pulled back."

It was a humane request. Six hours in any one position can cause almost unbearable pain. Your hands crossed at the wrist and lashed behind you when lying on a cement floor becomes a form of torture.

Gil slunk out and got into the car while the big fellow taped Flo's wrists - in front of her. He did the same for me, perhaps in deference to the injuries I'd sustained.

"I'm going to sit between you two in the back seat," he said. "I'm going to gag you and put a hood over your heads so you won't see where we're going or where you've been. As long as you keep still we'll have a nice ride. Okay?"

He was like a stern fond father explaining how it would be to his small children on the way to the beach. Only this wasn't a holiday outing. There was no picnic waiting for us at the end of the journey. Not likely.

He retaped Flo's ankles, gagged her and slipped a brown hood over her head. He gagged me too and put an identical hood over my head. It smelled of disinfectant. Even in the bright light of the garage I could see nothing through it. He helped us into the car one at a time, leaned across me and shut the door and then said, "Let's be on our way."

The driver got out of the car and turned off the lights. I heard the garage door open after he got back into the car which meant he controlled the door from inside. He backed out. The door came down again. We moved down a long smooth drive and turned left onto a dirt road. I thought I caught the smell of cow manure. Was there a dairy farm there? Then we were on the highway.

"Don't raise your hands to your face," the big man said. "If you make any attempt to remove the gags I'll have to make you less comfortable. And if I tell you to slump down, be sure to get your heads well below the level of the windows immediately. I guess you understand that."

I'd been wondering about the possibility that someone might notice two hooded figures in the back of a powerful car. It would look more than a little supicious. That settled that.

I still didn't know what time it was, but the absence of almost all other traffic on the road made it seem probable that we were in the very early hours of the morning. Three AM perhaps.

Several times the big man put his hand on my shoulder - no doubt he did the same to Flo - and told us to slump down. I'd hear another car, or a truck, go by, and then we were allowed to sit up again. I pretended to go to sleep and the next time he said to get down I didn't move. His hand on my shoulder pulled me to him and shoved me to the floor with authority.

"Don't try that again," he said.

I didn't intend to.

It was impossible to determine anything about the direction in which we were traveling. The road surface was excellent. We moved at a good clip but nothing excessive. Once, I felt we were going around a rotary. As far as I could tell we didn't encounter any traffic lights. How long did we travel? I'd guess at twenty minutes, but bound and gagged and hooded and scared, who could tell?

For the final couple of miles, we were forced to lie on the floor. Then we pulled into a garage and I heard an overhead door come down as the motor was cut off.

Voices. Men's voices. Rough hands. Hood still in place, I was carried through some sort of passageway and set down on a hardwood floor. The hood was removed. So was the gag.

Flo and I were in a sort of game room. There was a pool table under shaded lights. In one corner was a card table. Lots of straight-backed chairs. A magazine rack. Knotty pine paneling on the walls. Oak parquet. Bar at one end. Two doors. Both closed. No windows.

Not a sound reached us from outside. The room seemed to be completely sound proof.

The big man had taken off our hoods after the two or three others had left. He was the one who removed our gags, too. There was a sofa against one wall. He helped Flo to her feet and carried her to the sofa and sat her there. Then he helped me to hobble there, too.

"You're on TV," he said, and pointed to the objective lens. "Stay right here. Both doors will be locked and guarded. If you try to move around at all, someone will come and restrain you. It's about two-thirty in the morning. When he gets up and is ready, the boss will come to pay you a visit. It may be a long wait. Better rest."

He gave us a two finger salute and went out and the silence coagulated around us. No traffic sounds. No jets. No radios. No voices. Not even the usual clicks and hummings of the relay systems every dwelling contains - air conditioning, heating, refrigeration. The lights over the pool table were in-

137

candescent - no low drone even there. They cast only a yellow circle around the table.

"Where are we?" Flo asked.

"I don't know," I said. "This could be the basement of an expensive home. I think we were carried through a passageway to get here from the garage. Just before we pulled in I thought I heard surf so we may be near the coast."

"What are they going to do with us?"

I didn't want to answer that question. "We'll have to wait and see," I said, but I thought that our chances were not good.

"They'll want to kill us." Flo said it without emotion. It was a logical conclusion. She didn't kid herself about anything.

I let my eyes circle the room. No doubt there were mikes placed here somewhere. If someone was watching the TV monitor and could also hear everything we said there wasn't much point in trying to get free. I could have removed the tape in a short time. And there were weapons handy - bottles, chair legs, cue sticks, billiard balls hard enought to split a human skull if thrown accurately. But if we moved at all someone would come. At least that's what we'd been told.

Flo must have been reasoning along the same lines. "It wouldn't do any good trying to loosen these tapes, would it," she said. "They'd see us."

"And they can hear us too, I'm sure," I added.

"Are you tired?"

"No."

"How bad is that wound?"

"Bearable. No permanent damage. Do you want to curl up here and sleep? I can scrunch into a corner."

"Not now. Thank you."

We sat there, our hands in our laps, like a couple in front of a TV set. Only it was the eye of the TV camera that was on us.

Twenty-four hours earlier we had been making love. Just the thought of it made my arms ache to be holding her again. She was one of those rare women who hold nothing back. No doubts about her own worth. No cover-up of real or imagined deficiencies. She knew who she was and gave herself totally to whatever occupied her. Not for a long time had I felt so strongly about someone.

For once, though, our thoughts had not gone in the same direction.

"Do you know that I have a daughter?" she asked.

"The Chief mentioned it," I said.

"This is the day I always go to see her. They say she waits for this day and talks about it constantly. She'll be heartbroken not to see me. She's mongoloid, you know."

I said I knew.

"We didn't realize anything was wrong at the beginning. I thought that she was a beautiful baby. If anyone else knew, they didn't tell me. When it was clear that she wasn't normal I think I loved her even more. Tom had the exact opposite reaction. He couldn't wait to have her sent away. It was the beginning of the end of everything between us.

"I kept her at home until she was five. Tom avoided her. He seemed to consider her condition a black mark against his reputation, his manhood. We argued constantly over putting her in an institution. Eventually, I had to give in.

"Everything I earn goes to pay her bills. Tom refuses to do anything for her. He has never gone to visit her. She used to ask where her Daddy was. Maybe by now she's forgotten him, but I suspect there is an awareness there of something missing.

"It's hard to tell. The prettiness of the infant disappeared long ago. She's graceless and loud and unlovely now, her tongue protruding, clumsy. But she runs stumbling to me each time I visit and holds me so hard it hurts and I know that being loved still by someone means more to her than anything else in this world. I can't bear to think of her disappointment today when I don't appear."

She was crying. No sobs. No choking up. Just a steady stream of tears overflowing her eyes, running on her face, dropping onto her blouse where a dark wet patch grew minute by minute.

It's not physical pain that is hardest to bear. It's the knowledge that we have failed someone we love.

"We'll get out of this, Flo. Somehow we'll get free."

"It's kind of you to say it." She tried to smile. "You make me believe almost anything is possible."

"There are a lot of hours left in the day. We'll get a break somewhere down the line. You'll see."

$\mathcal{I}$t was a long night, however, before the day even broke. And we couldn't see the dawn, nor was there any way to guess what time it was.

We dozed. We talked, off and on, in a desultory manner.

Without preliminaries, three men came through the door closest to us. First, was a solid muscle-bound brute wearing black corduroy pants, running shoes and a wool plaid shirt. A Smith and Wesson .38 was shoved inside his belt, in front.

The second man was even smaller than I, maybe five-six, frail the way a sick man is, sixty years old give or take five, very large black-rimmed glasses, dressed in a dark tailor-made suit. The boss. Salvatore Pancione himself.

The third individual was a twin of the first except that he carried a long-barreled pistol in a shoulder holster.

Sal sat in a metal chair in front of us, the two bodyguards on each side of him, arms crossed, faces without expression, no sign of intelligence there either.

"You have give me a lotta trouble," Sal said.

His voice was labored and rasping, the voice of a man who has smoked constantly all his life and given it up too late, when the cancer has already taken root.

"If it wasn for you, Paula wouldn be caught." He pronounced it Pa-oo-la, *a l'Italiana.*

"Then you go to Ballantine an' he can' walk no more, prolly never be the same. How you find him?"

He was like an old crocodile before me, hardly moving, scarcely breathing, yellow wide-spaced teeth just showing in the straight bloodless line of his mouth, reptilian eyelids covering all but the iris.

I said, "One of the men who tried to burn Huck's barn was out of his mind before he died. He was burned all over his body. He mumbled a couple of names at the end. George Vale was one of them." It was a shot in the dark.

"You a liar," Sal said.

Bad shot.

"Mario never knew Ballantine by any other name. Only a very few of us know where he lives and what name he uses. Who tole you?"

This fragile near-sighted moribund ancient was not one you could fool.

"A cop told me."

"What cop? Not that Chief of police on Cape Cod?"

141

"A Boston cop. Ballantine's real name is Giorgio Valentino. He's got a record a mile long."

"An' the name Vale is not on that record. Now who tole you?"

"I wrote a letter to Ann Landers."

"You wasting my time." He turned to the bodyguard on his right. "Go get Gill," he ordered.

The other guard drew his pistol and clicked off the safety as his partner left the room. No one spoke for three minutes. Immobile, Flo sat beside me, jaws clenched.

Then Gill came in followed by the bodyguard. Someone had worked him over. One eye was closed. A corner of his mouth was torn. He was limping.

"You remember this lady?" Sal asked him.

Gill looked sideways at Flo. What was going on? "I wouldn't forget that one, Boss."

"How you like to take a roll on her?"

Gill wasn't sure he understood. I did.

"All right," I said. "Lug that slop bucket out of here and I'll tell you what you want to know."

Sal tipped his head to indicate that Gill should go. He was led out into the care of someone just outside. The door closed once more.

"Stan Butkowski told me," I said. "I found out that he and Ballantine went up for murder. Stan got the short end of it. I figured he'd talk. He did."

I'd promised Stan I wouldn't use his name. Now he was due for a clobbering. Another guilt package I'd be carrying for life - what was left of it. But wasn't Flo worth any number of Stan Butkowskis?

Sal nodded. "Something else you gonna tell me now. Porter is ready to sell. Seelye was ready before we started. Frank

Huck is weakening. The Porter property is held jointly - Thomas J. Porter et ux. How we gonna get the lady to sell?"

We were all watching Flo then. "I will never release my title to a single square inch of land to any corrupt contemptible creature like you," she said.

Sal moved his head a centimeter left, then a centimeter right. "Isn' that jus' like a woman? Always gotta be the watcha call it? The fly in the ointmen'. Well, I tell you something, *Signora*. In the ole country the fly get smushed. Plenty dumb women too, they don't know their place. Maybe that what it take to learn you a lesson. *Cabiche*?"

The message was clear. I'd been almost certain they intended to kill us. The only questions now were Where, and When, and How?

"You're overlooking something," I said. "If Mrs. Porter disappears, then nobody can get a clear title to the property you want until her estate has been probated. You might wind up with several other heirs, every one of them unwilling to sell to you."

He gave me a long icy look. "I am use' to dealing with stubborn people," he said. "Funny how often they change their mind."

"But probate is a long process, Sal. It can take years and years and you haven't got the time. You're almost dead now."

. Death was one official he couldn't buy off or intimidate. He didn't like the reminder. "You will still be dead sooner," he said.

He stood up. "Tonight you will both be taken out in a small boat. Is gonna to be a warm night, they say. All your clothes will be left on a quiet part of the beach. Neatly. Side by side. 'Skinny dipping they went,' people will assume. Only the water is getting cold now. Two bodies will be found next morning, or next afternoon. 'Lovers drown,' papers will write. End of opposistion. Pleasant dreams."

He left, one bodyguard preceding him, one following.

Minutes later, two other men appeared. There was a whole platoon quartered in this place it seemed. One held a gun on us. The other cut the tapes on our ankles. We were walked out of the game room, down a corridor, down a short flight of stairs and into a room similar to the storage shed we'd been in earlier.

The walls and the floor were cement. There was a drain in the middle of the floor. No window. Entrance to the room - and exit from it - was through double metal doors, one of which opened in, while the other opened out. Both had dead bolts. The ten-foot-high ceiling was padded. It looked like a torture chamber - a place where information was extracted, or punishment meted out.

Each of us was chained to a ring sunk in the concrete on opposite sides of the room. The two men left, closing and locking both doors. A single bulb in the ceiling was left on.

Twelve feet separated Flo and me. Our hands were still taped in front of us. Our legs were free. A steel band, three inches wide, went around our waists and locked behind us. There were four or five links in the chain that went from the steel band to a ring in the wall, not enough so we could sit, or lie down, just enough so we could stand free, or lean against the wall. As time went on it would become intolerable standing there, but for the moment it was painless.

I looked at every corner of the cell. No TV eye. I suspected that there was no mike either, but I wanted to be sure. Flo was watching me. I winked at her and raised a finger to my lips, the way you signal someone to be quiet.

"Look," I said in a stage whisper. "That dumb bozo didn't lock my bellyband." I rattled the chain. "I'm free. All I need to do is get the tape off my wrists and I'll see about setting you loose too."

"Shhh," Flo said. "Don't let them hear you." She'd understood. For several minutes we waited. Nothing happened. No one came. We could probably have set off firecrackers without being heard.

"I guess it's an improvement," Flo said. "They're not watching or listening, but how do you break an iron chain?"

I had an idea on that, but first I wanted to know if anyone was going to check on us from time to time.

It seemed likely that it was about nine in the morning. There could be twelve hours to wait before our rendezvous with the drowners.

I told Flo I thought we should play it dumb until someone came. That way we'd have some indication of how much time we had between check- ups.

"Suppose no one comes?" she asked.

"There's an organized set-up here," I said. "Even in county jails they check the inmates regularly. Someone will put a head in the door every hour or so."

I wasn't a bit sure of that, but it was a way to keep us optimistic. The trouble was, we had no way of measuring time. When I regained consciousness in the storage shed, my watch was gone, along with my wallet and everything else I had in my pockets. Flo hadn't had anything with her when she was nabbed. And she never wore a watch.

So time dragged. Standing in just one spot became uncomfortable. The tape on our wrists was tight and painful. No food or liquid had been given to us. I was used to a substantial breakfast. Better not think about that.

Flo stood across from me under the harsh light of the naked light bulb. She didn't slouch. Her back was straight. Sometimes she smiled at me. We were scheduled to be held under water in a few hours and drowned like unwanted cats, but she showed no sign of fear. She was thinking escape, just as I was. She was not one to give up.

It seemed like three but may only have been one hour when we heard the outer door open and then the one that opened in. A pale, pock-marked face peered first at Flo and then at me.

"Is everybody happy?" the man asked.

"How about a chair to sit on?" I said.

"No chairs. The management offers apologies."

"Or some food? And something to drink?"

"No comestibles, Sorry."

"Can't you do anything for us?" Flo asked.

"Just look in to see you ain't flowed the coop. Be good. Don't go 'way."

The door closed and we were alone again.

So he was the check-up man. He looked like a janitor, or handyman, to me, factotum of some sort. And we had a good hour or more between visits. That should be enough. Flo was looking to me.

"Let's go to work on this tape," I said.

I could see where the final strand had been pressed tight. With tongue and incisors and canines I got it loose and inch by inch began unwinding it. Flo started doing the same thing. It was an ordeal. The tape was heavy duty stuff and the adhesive was brutally strong. Where it was against bare skin it took the hairs right out by the roots when you pulled it free.

I yanked the last strip off and began massaging my wrists. My tongue and lips were bloody. I looked across at Flo. She had her hands free too. She'd been even quicker than I. Does that say something about the mouth and tongue of a woman?

146

Maybe her teeth were just sharper. She was watching me. "What next?" she asked.

I'd been working on that and wasn't sure. The steel band was tight enough to hurt. It had a series of ratchets on it so that when our jailers put it on us they fitted it to our different waists. Fat people would present a problem. Not us. When the band was tight it was locked into place. The hasp on the band and the last link on the chain in the wall were joined by a padlock of hardened steel that even a hacksaw couldn't cut.

Once, I'd watched a man at a circus get out of a web of steel bands and chains. He'd been stripped to a jock strap, though, and was covered with vaseline. He could have slipped out of what was on me in less than ten seconds. I knew I couldn't.

But I was able to turn inside the band and face the wall. If I'd had any kind of rudimentary tools I could have picked the lock, but that, too, was out.

One thing remained.

I put my hands against the wall. My feet too. Pushing out from the wall against the band at my waist, I was able to rotate, like a spider. After a turn and a half, the links in the chain allowed no further rotation. I was head down. I felt the band cutting into my right ribs and my left hip bone. I strained to turn a little further and felt something begin to give. Was it part of me, or was it a link in the chain? The injury to my left side was throbbing. The band was going to break a rib if I put any more pressure on it.

I reversed direction and got back on my feet. I took off my shirt and stuffed it inside the band in the places where I had been hurting most, a moment before. Then I pushed off from the wall again. Had there been anything to grab, any foothold or handhold, it would have been easy, but when I was head down and needed to increase the torsion on the links of the chain, I had nothing to grasp. So I tried one other thing.

I was standing on my hands but held erect by the chain. I extended my legs and let them fall clockwise as far as they could while I tried to scramble clockwise with my hands.

It worked. One link in the chain popped and I fell to the floor. The band was still locked around my middle. Two links from the chain dangled from it and clinked together when I moved. But I was mobile gain. I was free.

"Leverage," Flo said. "A simple matter of leverage. But it's the first time I've ever seen a human body become the lever."

"Now it's your turn," I said. "You don't mind if I stand you on your head?"

"There's nothing you would do that I would mind."

I crossed the room and held her close, for a moment, as close as our chastity belts would allow. She was warm against me. In the chill room, without my shirt on, my skin was clammy. Her good hands moved on my back and arms bringing blood and heat back to the surface. We could have stood holding each other indefinitely, but it was important not to lose time. Someone was going to come back to check on us again.

I used my shirt to pad the band around her waist. There was no need for her to turn inside the band to face the wall. I braced my feet and took her waist in crossed arms and spun her once.

"The human pinwheel," she said, when she was on her feet again.

"Now for the hard part," I said. "Are you ready?"

She nodded.

I took her in crossed arms again and turned her gently until she was head down and could be turned no further.

148

"Hold my ankles," I said. "I'll take hold of the band now so it won't be cutting into your sides too much. Now, pull against my legs in the same direction that I'm twisting."

The chain let go and she was free. I let her down slowly.

"Nothing broken?"

"Nothing broken," she said. "Not even bruised. Here. Put your shirt on again. It wouldn't do to escape and then come down with pneumonia."

How much time had passed? When we were just waiting, it had inched forward, every minute an eternity. Now that we expected to see the little guy with the pock-marked face more or less regularly, time could be flying.

"Get on my shoulders," I said. "We've got to unscrew that light bulb so it will be harder to see us when our friend returns."

Those strong thighs against my cheeks, her ankles in my hands, I stood under the one light bulb in the room. She slipped off her blouse and used it to protect her fingers from the hot glass. Abruptly, we were in total darkness again.

"Leave the bulb in the socket," I said. "That way we can say it must have burned out."

I crouched down and she got onto her own feet again. She returned to her place by the wall and resumed her position there, hands crossed in front of her as if still chained in place. I stood by the door, where it would hide me for a split second as it opened, and waited. There would be some light from the corridor. I was going to get just one chance. If I muffed it, the alarm would be out.

Seconds crept into minutes. In other rooms the hands of clocks were making their way around a circular hour. I counted slowly to sixty and then started over. Did I do it ten times. I lost track.

Then I heard a key in the outside door. It opened and a key was put into the lock next to me. Flo heard it too.

"Thank goodness you came back," she said, as the inside door swung open. "Our light bulb has burned out. Can you..."

His head was inches from mine. I grabbed a handful of coarse hair and yanked and got my other hand over his mouth before he started to yell. I put my right arm around his neck from behind, cutting off the blood supply to his head. In only minutes he was out.

Flo ripped his shirt into strips. We tied his hands and feet with it. There were pieces of tape left for that purpose too, and for gagging him. Then we stepped into the corridor, locking both doors behind us with the keys our jailer had been holding in his hand.

To our right was the way we had been brought in. To our left, ten feet away, was a half-open door. I moved to it and looked in. It was where our former jailer had been stationed.

Three TV monitors were on one wall. On one, four burly men were shooting pool in the game room. Two of them were the ones who had taken us to the place where we had been locked up. Were the two others the ones who were scheduled to drown us?

The second monitor showed an empty driveway. Maybe it was a view from the front door to screen anyone arriving here.

The third was the one that caught my attention.

Salvatore Pancione had his back to us. He was seated at a wide desk. One bodyguard was at his side, the other was to the rear. The camera was pointed at a man in a business suit who looked familiar. I knew his face. Flo did too. "It's a state rep from Barnstable County," she said. He was talking. The sound of his voice came to us softly.

"I don't want to know what you're planning," he said. "I don't want to know what you've done. I'll see that those records disappear. That's all."

"An' you won' keep any duplicates for yourself," Sal said, in his emery paper voice.

"Look. We don't trust each other. Okay. But neither of us can afford to hurt the other. I know that. You know that. Don't worry."

I realized that the whole scene was being video-taped. There were racks full of tapes all around us. They had dates and names on them. Flo had found a canvas tote bag. She was selecting tapes and putting them into the bag.

There was a key board next to a cheap desk. I found the key for the padlocks that held the steel bands around our waists. What a relief it was to get out of them!

In the center drawer of the desk was a ledger. It was a record of all visitors - dates, times, and VT written by each entry if a tape had been made. I handed it to Flo to put in the bag. In the same drawer was a .357 magnum. I checked. It was loaded. We were in business again. All we had to do now was get out, alive.

A door to the left of the three monitors opened onto a stairway going up. I led the way, gun in hand. We emerged into a gleaming kitchen. A digital clock over a stainless steel sink read 10:43. No one was in sight, but a wall oven was turned on and what looked like a rib roast in it was just beginning to simmer. Too bad we wouldn't be staying for lunch.

I tried to figure how many people might be in the house. There were the four in the game room, the two bodyguards, Sal and the state rep. That made eight. Where was Gill, and the powerful guy who had brought us to this place? Maybe there was a cook and a groundsman, too. You might say that we were outnumbered.

From the kitchen window all I could see was about eighty feet of open lawn, then trees and a section of driveway leading down and away. This was the rear of the house. The monitor that had shown the front drive - if that's what it was - hadn't revealed any other buildings either. We were in a large expensive house on an extensive estate. It was probably the South Shore home of Salvatore Pancione. Were we in Scituate? Marshfield? Hingham? If it was any of those, other dwellings ought to be relatively near. The same was true of roadways. If we could get out of the house and across the lawns we'd have a chance, but the minute we were discovered in the house our chances fell away to near zero.

Logically, a kitchen connects with a dining room. A dining room with a family room. The room where Sal was talking with the rep could be a den off the livingroom. This was the ground floor. Bedrooms would be up one more flight. Was anyone else up there?

Cautiously, I pushed the swinging door into what I hoped would be a dining room. That's what it was, and an open arch revealed another room beyond it with large sofas and comfortable chairs and a fireplace.

The oven had been set at 350 degrees. I pushed it up to 600 and led Flo into the room with the sofas. I put her in back of one by a bay window and I crouched behind a walnut chest where I could cover both sides of the room. Voices were coming from a door on my right. Sal was in there.

We waited. The front door was directly across from me. Glass on each side of it gave a view of the driveway I'd seen on the second TV monitor.

Little by little, the smell of meat beginning to burn reached us. At first it was a good smell mingled with a garlic flavor, but quickly it turned acrid and a gray haze crept into the room.

The voices in Sal's study got louder. His door opened. I stayed down and out of sight.

"Something burning." It was Sal's voice. "Vito, go look the kitchen."

I saw one of the bodyguards cross the room and go into the kitchen. I stood up. The second bodyguard was in the doorway to Sal's study. "Don't move." I said to him. Sal was two paces in front of him. The state rep just to the rear.

But the second bodyguard started to draw the long-barreled pistol. I shot him dead center through the chest. He went over backwards, blood spurting from the wound, legs and arms jerking.

Vito came through the swinging door from the kitchen, gun out. The death throes of his partner caught his eye first and may have saved me. I had time to put a bullet through his right side before he looked my way. In spite of the wound, he was able to turn toward me and raise his gun. My second shot blew a hole through the middle of his face and sent a hunk of his skull and a streamer of brains splattering onto the still-swinging door. He folded into a heap on the floor like a bundle of wet laundry.

The state rep was looking from one body to the next and his face was green. I thought he was about to throw up. Instead, he fainted.

Sal hadn't moved. "Lock your fingers behind your head," I told him. I stepped in back of him.

I heard footsteps, at least two people pounding up the stairs.

I held Sal in front of me with my left arm. He was skin and bones and where his hands brushed against my face he was icy cold.

Two of the pool players came along the hallway in front of us. Each was carrying a gun.

"Drop the weapons," I said.

The one in the lead did as he was told but the other one moved behind his buddy and fired. The bullet went through my left forearm and entered Sal's chest. Sal sagged against me.

I shot at the head of the man with the gun and saw the side of his face come apart. It ruined his aim. His second shot went into the wall above and behind me. His buddy threw himself on the floor, arms extended, face down.

I put my next shot through the gut of the man with half a face who was still standing. He collapsed. Blood gushed from his mouth. He lay on the floor, thrashing, but he wasn't dangerous anymore.

I heard someone else in the hallway. Smoke was filling the room. The smell of cordite mingled with the odor of that good roast burning. I could barely make out the shape approaching across from me. I fired and missed. The searing pain in my injured arm was affecting me.

To my left a gun exploded and the man coming at me fell backwards and wasn't going to move ever again.

I heard a car, wheels spinning, take off down the drive. Then it was quiet, a big heavy deadly quiet.

Flo got to her knees behind the sofa. I saw that she was holding a gun. She put it down on a table and stared at it and held her hands against her sides wiping them on her dress, shaking all over.

I noticed I was still clutching Sal. He was dead. I let go of him. His emaciated body slumped to the floor.

The one uninjured gunman, lying face down on a rug, said, "I'm not moving. Don't shoot."

My legs were about to go out from under me. "I'm going to ask you one question," I said to him. "Give me the wrong answer and you're dead. What's the address here?"

He told me.

I looked at Flo. She was still trembling. "Go into Sal's office," I said to her, as gently as I could. "There must be a phone in there. Dial Operator. Get the police here. Ask for an ambulance, too."

I had to sit down. I'd lost a lot of blood. It looked as if an artery had been severed above my wrist. When I held my arm tight against my chest the bleeding slowed, but I was getting woozy. The room began turning. One corner seemed to be lifting into the air...

$\mathcal{R}$eturning to a conscious state in a hospital bed was not a new esperience for me. It was pleasant, in a way. One more time I wasn't dead.

I didn't open my eyes right away. There was enough morphine in me to create a sense of floating, a lightness relieved of pressure, a high of not caring. Nothing really mattered.

Then I remembered Flo. I sat up.

"Hey. Easy."

It was Flo. She'd been dozing beside me. She was safe. She was here. I sank back into the pillows. She put both hands on my right arm. My left was immobilized.

"Are you okay?" I asked.

"Untouched, physically," she said.

I sought her eyes. There was a new seriousness in her. "You shot a man who was about to kill me."

She nodded.

"You picked up a gun that had skidded across the floor."

"Yes."

"I owe you my life."

"I already owed you mine."

"I'm sorry - sorry you had to kill."

"I did it without thinking. I'm not sure I could do it again, no matter what the circumstances. I wouldn't want to. I'd stop to think, another time. Then it would probably be too late."

I raised my hand and touched her cheek. "You said it about someone else the day I met you," I said. "It's true of you too. You are one woman in a million."

An MD entered the room. "So," he said. "Back with the living again."

"How much damage is there?" I asked.

"You were lucky. The bullet passed between the radius and the ulna without touching either bone. Tore up a lot of tissue and ligaments, though. We repaired most of it, but you'll probably have to come back for corrective surgery later in order to recover full use of the hand.

"You lost a lot of blood - almost no pulse when you got to us. This lady gave you enough to keep you going."

"She's my type, I guess."

"Blood type, you mean."

"That too," I said.

"Goddamn," he said. "I'll be Goddamned," he said, and left.

Flo was smiling. It was a good smile. I was feeling much better already.

"Tell me what happened after I passed out," I asked.

"You were out cold on the armchair when I came back from calling the police. I saw you were bleeding terribly so I wrapped your arm in an antimacasser as tightly as I dared. It stopped most of the bleeding, but you were mighty gray for a black man.

156

"The gunman on the rug just kept saying, 'I'm not moving, I'm not moving. Don't shoot.' I can't help wondering how he ever got into that line of work.

"The state rep recovered consciousness, took one look around, and passed out again. I sat there praying no one else would appear. No one did.

"The police arrived and you know, they rang the bell and stood outside waiting. I had to step over all those corpses and the rep and open the door for them. The ambulance was there. I had blood all over me so they took me along with you."

"You've had a chance to get cleaned up."

"One of the nurses here had some extra things and let me borrow them."

"You're beautiful, Flo," I said.

"I'm glad you think so."

"We need to do some serious talking."

"Haven't things been serious enough already?"

"You know what I mean."

"Yes." She leaned over and kissed me. That was when Huck came into the room. He stood in the doorway and waited until we looked up at him."

"They tell me you'll be out of here by tomorrow," he said. He came over and shook my good hand. "We owe a lot to you. There's no way to thank you enough."

"You can take care of the medical bills," I said.

"That's already arranged. Any extra surgery too. And you'll have a new car. Whatever you pick out yourself."

"Can you take Flo to visit her daughter? It's not too late, is it?"

"That's one of the main reasons I had for driving up here," he said.

*A*fter they left, I'd only been alone for minutes when the Chief walked in. He looked at me and shook his head. "A scratched arm you've got," he said, "and the other team has enough injured to fill a ward here and enough dead to fill two tiers at the morgue. The Hell you do it, Jeeter?"

"I had help this time, Chief."

"Mrs. Porter?"

"She took out one of them."

"Lucky for you she did, if I've got it straight."

"I wouldn't be here if she hadn't. She saved me from bleeding to death, too."

He cocked his head. "I hadn't heard about that. Anyway, the local authorities are going to want a statement from you. Then there'll be a hearing. Did you happen to know that there was a tape running and it recorded just about all the mayhem?"

I'd forgotten about the tapes. "You mean the audio part caught the whole thing?"

"Almost all of it."

He hadn't needed to tell me that. Probably shouldn't have. It would be a way of corroborating my statement when I made it.

"I owe you one, Chief."

"No you don't. You've put a big operation out of business and saved all of us an endless headache. Salvatore Pancione is gone and just about every pie he had a finger in is going off the shelf, thanks to the way you infiltrated his headquarters."

I liked that 'infiltrated' but I didn't deserve it.

"Getting bushwhacked and abducted is what I did. It wasn't all that clever of me."

"Yeah. Well, it's results that count. Tell me, were you and Mrs. Porter chained to the wall in that cellar dungeon?"

"For a couple of hours."

"They found a little guy with terrible acne tied up in there. He'd been wanted for years. He's a safe cracker, a specialist on locks. He said there was no way you could have got free unless you had tools. And he said you and the lady had been frisked from head to toe. How did you do it?"

"Just one of my little secrets. I didn't pick any locks. I broke the chain."

"How?"

"If you put an iron bar through one link in a chain that's fixed in place, and then you twist, it'll break every time."

"And where were you hiding an iron bar, up your backside?"

"In a manner of speaking."

Slowly, he shook his head. He was still shaking when three other men came in.

One was an assistant DA, the second was a technician who set up a mike and tape recorder. The third was a stenographer. They took my statement and then the DA wanted to go over some details.

"You say that the third man you shot was the one who killed Pancione."

"That's right."

"Why would he shoot at you when you were using Pancione as a shield?"

"I'm not sure."

"You thought he wouldn't shoot."

"That was a logical assumption."

"But he didn't hesitate."

"He fired point blank."

"Do you think he wanted to kill his boss?"

"It's possible. Sal was a sick man. He looked like a dying man, to me. The man who shot him - and got me in the arm doing it - may have thought he could take over the operation. His buddy - the one that chose to lie on the floor and not move - might have some answers."

"And the two that brought you and Mrs. Porter to Sal's mansion - would you recognize pictures of them?"

"Of course."

He had eight mug shots with him. He laid them out on the sheet next to me.

"This is the one they called Gill," I said, picking up one of the photos. "He was the driver."

"You're sure?"

"Positive."

"This guy was released on good behavior only a month ago. Francis Gilliam. He'd been at Bridgewater - aggravated sexual assault, not guilty by reason of insanity, a record of sex crimes going back more than twenty years. And they let him out!"

"How did you happen to have his photo?"

"These are all recent Massachusetts escapees or releases."

"The big man who was with Gill wouldn't be one of those," I said. "I think he's been with the organization for quite a while. I suspect that he's part of the clinic - he and the nurse we caught on the Cape."

160

The Chief had been quiet up to then. "An anonymous informant left me some phone numbers a day ago," he said. "I ran down the addresses. One was Sal's place. Three look like loan shark centers. And one is in Westwood. A private home, in appearance, but it could be the clinic."

"A colonial style dwelling, four white columns out front?" the DA asked.

"That's it. How'd you know?"

"We've been watching it for months. We knew something was going on there, but we weren't sure what. We have warrants ready. I'll go take care of that one now."

His assistants packed up their gear and all departed.

My arm was starting to throb. As long as there was no infection, that was probably a good sign.

The Chief was watching me. "Let them put you to sleep again," he said, "but first you should know that the state representative was in cahoots with Selwyn Rose <u>and</u> guess who?"

"Seelye," I said.

His eyebrows went up.

"It had to be," I said. "Seelye wanted to sell. Needed to, I bet. He's small time with dreams of another order. I've seen his type before. It's funny how knowledge of the law - those laws that are supposed to be there to protect us - can corrupt the ones who work with it. Seelye's practice was almost all torts - using the law to obtain exaggerated settlements for minor losses and injuries. I hope he gets put away for a long time."

"Your Mrs. Porter picked out some video tapes that may put him out of circulation for many years. He'll be disbarred for starters."

That possessive pronoun wasn't there unintentionally. No one should ever underestimate small town cops.

161

"Maybe we'll be seeing more of you," he said, as he got up to go.

"Maybe you will," I said.

Flo came up to Boston a week later. I was almost back to normal. There was going to be some tendon repair in another couple of weeks so I was taking it easy in my apartment on Revere Street.

She had a suitcase with her. She stepped inside and set it down.

"What took you so long?" I asked.

"I had to make up my mind."

"And you did?"

She nodded.

"You're sure you want to take your chances with me?"

"We'll try it out for a while," she said. "Maybe I'll just never let go."